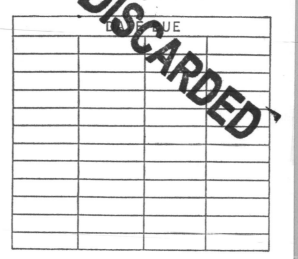

COMMUNITY
Reflections on a Tragic Ideal

GLENN TINDER/ # COMMUNITY
Reflections on
a Tragic Ideal

Louisiana State University Press
Baton Rouge and London

Designer: Patricia Douglas Crowder
Typeface: VIP Bembo
Typesetter: G & S Typesetters, Inc.

LIBRARY OF CONGRESS CATALOGING IN PUBLICATION DATA

Tinder, Glenn E.
    Community: Reflections on a tragic ideal.

    1. Community.   I. Title.
HM131.T53   301.34   79–19821
ISBN 0–8071–0659–3

To Evan

". . . here we have no continuing city . . ."
HEBREWS 13:14

CONTENTS

PREFACE

It is important for readers to bear in mind what is indicated in the subtitle. This book is a set of distinct inquiries, not a systematic work. I do not try to set forth a comprehensive, organized theory. Readers who look for such a theory are apt to misunderstand the meaning of the book.

The separateness of the inquiries is not accidental, however. It is not the result of having written a number of occasional pieces that happened all to bear on a single subject. Rather, it expresses my conviction that systematic political theory, although often useful, always falsifies, since reality itself is not systematic. The reality with which these inquiries are concerned is, I believe, particularly resistant to systematic treatment. Community and the trials it imposes on human beings in history are not readily understood through systematic theories.

Moreover, the separateness of the inquiries is not only deliberate; it is intended to further the communication of a single theme—a theme that cannot, I think, be embodied in any single concise and comprehensive statement but that may gradually take shape in the minds of readers who do not look for a unified theoretical structure. The lack of *systematic* unity, then, does not imply a lack of *substantial* unity.

This implies that the inquiries are closely related even though distinct. What I say in one may clarify what I mean in another, and each inquiry should be read with a consciousness of its setting in the whole series of reflections. The order of the inquiries has been a matter of prolonged and careful consideration and is intended to convey something of my overall theme.

It may be well to add that, so far as I can determine, these inquiries are without ideological as well as without systematic unity. I frequently take issue with radicalism, and I am afraid that in consequence I will be classified as a conservative. But I do not consider myself a conservative and do not think that any discriminating conservative, in the tradition either of Edmund Burke or of Adam Smith, will accept me as an ally. Indeed, some readers may object to my emphatically perfectionist approach to social and political realities: I believe that even though we cannot *make* society what it ought to be, it is essential, for maintaining both our personal independence from the established order and our sense of man's nobility, not to *forget* what society ought to be. It may seem that I must be some sort of liberal. Perhaps I am, for I am sympathetic with a number of liberal positions, especially on day-to-day issues. But the tacit theme of these inquiries—the theme I hope is evoked without being stated—is distant from the liberal ethos.

For a book that promises to place heavy demands on the sympathy and discernment of the reader, it may seem that a more explicit and lengthy introduction would be appropriate. Such an introduction is provided, I believe, by the first inquiry, "Community: The Tragic Ideal." There an effort is made to glance over the whole terrain that these reflections explore.

Three of these inquiries are revised versions of articles that have previously appeared in print. The first, "Community: The Tragic Ideal," appeared originally in *The Yale Review*, LXV (Summer, 1976). The fourth, "In Defense of Pure Tolerance," appeared in *Polity*, VI (Summer, 1974); and the last, "Beyond Tragedy: The Idea of Civility," in *The American Political Science Review*, LXVIII (June, 1974). I wish to thank the editors of all three periodicals for permission to republish.

COMMUNITY
Reflections on a Tragic Ideal

I / COMMUNITY: THE TRAGIC IDEAL

The Communal Dream

Perhaps no term in the current vocabulary of politics glows with so many favorable connotations as does "community." The most powerful radical writings, such as those of Herbert Marcuse and Frantz Fanon, delineate visions of community; liberal reformers typically find the origins of social evils like crime and poverty in the breakdown of community; and even conservatives do not generally oppose the aspiration to community but only the notion that attaining community requires radical change.

I shall question this consensus. When the ideal of community is adhered to with consistency and determination it is a source of serious and irresolvable tensions. This does not mean that the ideal misrepresents human needs and desires, or that it should be wholly given up. It does mean, however, that the ideal needs to be reflected on with some care, for it demands far more of us than most of us realize.

Let us try to clarify, at the outset, what we are discussing. The term "community" has, of course, more than one meaning. Sometimes it merely denotes a town or a city and has no moral connotations. Here, however, we are concerned with an ideal—an ideal of perfect unity, such as that represented in the writings of Plato and Jean Jacques Rousseau. When Plato outlined a polity made up of three classes, led by those in whom philosophical reason was the dominant faculty, he was trying to prescribe for every human type its proper place in the social order. Thus in Plato's ideal city, people would be united according to the demands of their own essence; social unity would not infringe upon, but would be the very condition of, personal wholeness. And when Rousseau discussed the "general will," he was trying to formulate the concept of a social will that would be identical with the innermost will of every member of society. Obeying such a will, the citizen would be simultaneously at one with others and wholly free. Both Plato and Rousseau envisaged societies that would join people as full and authentic human beings, not as parts trimmed and shaped to fit into an external order. The perfect harmony of whole and part is the key to the ideal of community.

No wonder that ideal has been alluring, for it promises both self-realization and an end to loneliness. Every major historical period has responded to the lure of community by creating a simulacrum and myth of community—in ancient times, the *polis*; in the Middle Ages, the universal church; in the modern world, the nation-state. The present revolutionary era has joined this historical procession with its own dream of ideal unity—communism.

Community is not only alluring, however, it is also unattainable. Man is not capable of community—not, at least, in any full and stable form. No doubt relationships of communal quality can be realized occasionally and in limits by a family, a town, a university, or even a nation. But no historical institution can be purely and simply a community.

The unattainability of community (not, be it noted, the undesirability of community) seems to me a crucial and neglected truth. It accounts for the dangerous character of the ideal. Full community is unattainable partly because man is a natural being; he lives in space and time, and he dies. To a surprising extent man's spatial, temporal, and mortal nature is ignored in writings on community. Karl Marx, for example, while prepared to overturn a civilization for the sake of community, never seriously reflected on the alienation that is inseparable from space, time, and death. Perhaps these conditions are so elemental they are taken for granted; perhaps they are too discouraging to be readily faced. Yet they are insuperably in the way of man's communal aspirations. Every association is spread out in space, eroded continually by time, and doomed by the mortality of its participants.

Even so, our natural capacity for community is often far in excess of our moral capacity. The tendency of every person to subordinate everything to his own pleasure and preeminence—a tendency that is subtle and enduring, although often disguised—frequently forecloses whatever communal possibilities nature offers.

The natural and moral obstacles to community are easily understood. This is not the case, however, with a third and final obstacle—one that may be called "axiological," since it has to do with value. The value in question is that of persons.

Willingness to enter into community depends on respect for other potential participants, and respect depends on a perception of value; this is how the question of value becomes involved with that of community. We respect people for their natural qualities—for their intelligence, their personal charm, and so forth. We also respect them for their moral qualities, such as honesty and kindliness. If our respect for others is determined wholly by their natural and moral qualities, however, the ideal of community is in trouble. This in part is because people are drastically unequal in the degree to which they command respect; people of good judgment ordinarily hold only a few in highest esteem. In addition, however, respect that is proportioned to natural and moral qualities must be severely limited in relation to everyone without exception. To say that man is spatial, temporal, and mortal, after all, is to say that he is finite, and this implies that the natural values he embodies are limited both in degree and duration. No one is more than relatively and temporarily intelligent, or skillful, or handsome. Likewise no one is more than relatively and temporarily good. If there are any who achieve moral perfection they are so rarely encountered in daily life as to be irrelevant to the problem of community. In sum, no one commands more than qualified respect. The communal impulse, capable of fulfillment only with those one respects and only in proportion to one's respect for them, is correspondingly inhibited.

This difficulty did not arise in the Christian ages of the past because a person was thought not to be identical with his natural or his moral—and sinful—being. Respect for every individual was called forth by his eternal destiny. But today not many are disposed to appeal from man's observable, worldly identity to an identity visible only to the eyes of faith. The problem of respect is therefore serious. That we are scarcely aware of it may be because, as Miguel de Unamuno charged, we are "spiritual parasites," retaining Christian values without Christian faith.[1]

Indicating the gravity of the problem is the fact that a writer of Fyodor Dostoevsky's stature centered his life's work on it. All of Dostoevsky's major novels had to do primarily with the catastrophic disruption of human relationships that he saw as necessarily following the decline of Christianity. To appreciate the problem, however, we need not anticipate events so extreme and disastrous as those depicted by Dostoevsky. Those who find their respect for human beings shaken on taking fully into account their finitude, mortality, and self-centeredness will not necessarily permit themselves, as did Raskolnikov, to murder people, nor will they necessarily, like Peter Verkhovensky, engage in nihilistic revolt. They may simply withhold themselves as far as they can from human contact. They may, like some of the most spiritual and moral of ancient pagans, idealize communities composed of classes sharply divided on the basis of natural and moral worth. Even at best, however, in approaching others they must be fastidious, severely discriminating, and—since the possibilities of community even at best are so narrow—regretful.

In summary, community is unattainable because of obstacles that are natural, moral, and axiological. These obstacles, arising from man's nature and ontological situation, cannot be surmounted within the limits of earthly and historical existence. This will become more fully apparent in the following pages. But one implication of this condition deserves immediate consideration: that so little, measured by our aspirations, can be accomplished through action.

The Failure of Action

Modern peoples, especially Americans, have often been exuberantly confident in their powers of action. Every reality is potentially within the scope of human control—so, at least, many have felt with the progress of technology. But no devices of action can overcome the obstacles to community. The empire of space and time can be resisted, but no conceivable course of action can lift human beings above finitude and mortality. Moral progress can be sought through educa-

1. Miguel de Unamuno, *Tragic Sense of Life*, trans. J. E. Crawford Flitch (New York: Dover Publications, 1954), 27.

tion, but no educational techniques bring assured results, and all efforts at moral improvement are adversely affected by the moral impurity inevitably involved in the effort itself. And in any case community cannot be an immediate object of action: if human beings are in essence free, then they cannot be deliberately united from without. The ideal of community drives the pragmatic mind to exasperation and hopelessness.

But if community is unreachable, why have human beings sought it so persistently? Why has every age produced its own distinctive institutional and theoretical image of community? Beyond the answers suggested above—that the obstacles are so well-known as to be taken for granted and so discouraging as to repel close attention—one motive is almost certainly pride. It is unpleasant to acknowledge our finitude and mortality, our moral imperfection, and the dubiousness of our claims to respect. While it may be entertaining briefly to toy with despair, in the long run we give credence to philosophies that reassure and exalt us.

Aside from the influence of familiarity, fear, and pride, however, there is an explanation for our inveterate communal hopes that is particularly important for understanding why the ideal of community is so troublesome. The persistence of the communal dream indicates that the ideal is valid—not as a representation of historical possibilities, but as an imperative of human nature. Even though community is unattainable, the longing for community expresses the essence of humanity. A person reaches fullness of being only in the company of others. It may be objected that what is closest to the human heart is not community but freedom. What would be the worth of freedom, however, without relationships? You desire freedom, presumably, in order to be yourself. But to be yourself you must enter into relationships; you must make friends, carry on a vocation, live in a certain place. These relationships, filled out and harmonized, constitute a community. This suggests that freedom is found only in community and that man is a communal being.

If so, then the obstacles to community do not merely place unpleasant limits on the satisfaction of our desires. They create a conflict between our condition and our essence. It begins to be apparent why it is appropriate to speak of community as a tragic ideal. Also, it becomes understandable that we are led repeatedly to vest exaggerated hopes in abortive communal strategies.

As often noted, political programs designed to produce community tend in fact to produce the opposite of community. The realization of community requires freedom, equality, and democracy—typical goals of leftists in their efforts to create a more communal America. Yet if human beings are only objects existing in space and time, and are perversely desirous of dominating those about them, then they can and must be constrained if they are to unite, and society must be organized in hierarchies of power. The result at its most benign may be an institution such as a New England town meeting—an assemblage appearing to be wholly democratic but in fact often carefully controlled by an able and public-spirited minority. The result at its most sinister may be a totalitarian dictatorship; here rulers undertake not just the traditional tasks of governance but the transformation of man, in order that his condition and his essence may correspond. Action in behalf of community can in this way bring nearly total alienation.

The Failure of Theory

Less often noted than the failure of communal action is the self-defeating character of much communal theory. Even ideas rebel, as it were, lending an anticommunal character to ostensibly communal theories. To understand what happens we must survey the basic strategies that communal theorists employ. Each major aspect of the human situation calls forth a typical strategic response.

1. SPACE. The ideal of community becomes that of the small and intimate association—the city-state, the village commune. Space, so far as possible, is excluded. Aristotle employed this strategy in prescribing a *polis* small enough to be surveyed in a glance. Modern radical thought, from Rousseau to the present, repeatedly recurs to the ideal of the face-to-face, "spaceless" society.

2. TIME. The ideal of a timeless society was delineated in *The Republic*. Plato was hypersensitive to the alienation implicit in time, and he depicted the history of the ideal state as a process of disintegration. He apparently envisioned a state as changeless as the eternal forms on

which his metaphysical thinking was centered. Conservatives typically share, in varying degrees, the platonic horror of time.

3. DEATH. Philosophers of community have often met the challenge of death by granting to some impersonal, undying reality an importance prior to that of the mortal individual. For Aristotle, this prior reality was the *polis* and beyond the *polis* the basic order of being; for Rousseau it was the state and the moral law; for Marx it was the human race in its full creative power. The common notion that dying must be natural and easy when it concludes a fulfilling life reflects a strategy of this kind: over against the all-enshrouding finality of death is invoked joyful, although merely generic, life.

4. EGOISM. To the charge that man is irremediably selfish, communal philosophy often answers that human nature is infinitely plastic. In the view of radicals, the evil in man is a consequence, rather than a cause, of the evil circumstances surrounding him. Hence man can be made unselfish and communal. Cooperative societies, in the Marxist vision, will give rise to cooperative human beings.

5. THE PROBLEM OF RESPECT. Here two different strategies are employed. One is to discover an actual or conceivable elite whose members embody the perfect dignity and worth lacking in human beings on the average. Full community is of course possible only within the elite, but partial community can be realized in society at large if absolute power is possessed by the elite. This was the strategy of Plato. The alternative is to construe man's dignity as a quality he has alienated but can recover. Thus Ludwig Feuerbach argued that man has lost his glory by bestowing it all on a fiction, on God; through atheism, however, man might reclaim his divinity.[2]

These strategies have marked out the main pathways of communal thought. Each of them, however, involves a betrayal of the ideal of community—and thus of man in his essence.

1. A "spaceless society" necessarily excludes all but a handful of the human race, and such exclusiveness must be measured not only in terms of numbers but in terms of genius and variety as well. Proponents of small societies usually recommend some form of federalism,

2. See Ludwig Feuerbach, *The Essence of Christianity*, trans. George Eliot (New York: Harper & Brothers, 1957).

thus acknowledging that the communal ideal does not allow human beings to be contented within a city-state or a village commune but draws them toward the unity of all mankind. But the concept of federalism only blurs the unresolved dilemma. So far as federal integration is effective personal intimacy is lost, whereas uncompromising defense of intimate groups implies a complete rejection of larger associations. The requirements of community are recognized not only in the Aristotelian *polis* but also in the Stoic *cosmopolis*.

2. If the "spaceless society" excludes most of the human race, the "timeless society" excludes a crucial human capacity, that of creativity. Man in his creativity is a source of change, of historical time. Hence a political effort to eliminate change entails the suppression of man in his essence. The remorselessness of this logic is dramatized by the fact that so towering a spiritual figure as Plato could idealize a censorious and closed society.

3. As for meeting death by invoking some impersonal and undying reality that is supposedly prior to the individual, it may be said simply that if the death of the individual is insignificant, so is the individual himself. Efforts to draw the sting from death usually imply that the individual is derivative and replaceable. But where there are no individuals, neither is there community. It is not accidental that Marxism has become a philosophy for totalitarian and murderous political regimes. Although Marx himself evidently sensed the dignity of individuals, in Marx's philosophy the primary reality and value is the species and not the individual.

4. It may seem that viewing man as potentially sinless cannot be so abortive as are these other philosophical strategies. Does it not express a wholesome trust? In truth, the idea that human beings are fundamentally good and innocent is surprisingly treacherous. It leads almost inevitably to an effort, potentially bloody, to identify and suppress those responsible for the evil all around us. Since the world is filled with injustice and suffering, if man generically is innocent then a few must be peculiarly culpable. This is the logic underlying the obsessive condemnation of capitalism and capitalists in Marxist thought. But this logic is not confined to Marxist thought; it is evident in the ferocious anti-Communism of traditionally optimistic Americans, and it has no doubt played a part in the persecution of the Jews. A seemingly

generous exculpation of all thus prompts the sweeping condemnation of a class, a nation, or a race.

5. The impossibility of reaching community by dividing elites from masses is plain. Such a strategy is self-defeating, even despairing, for it begins with a decree of separation. More plausible, at first glance, is the argument employed by Feuerbach—that human beings have a dignity and worth they have bestowed upon, but can reclaim from, an unreal god. The plausibility, however, vanishes on examination. Feuerbach was speaking of the human species and not of individuals; the dignity to be reclaimed belonged to universal man and not to every human being.

We have now reached a vantage point from which we can survey the terrain over which these reflections have led us and can consider the principal question to which we have been brought: how to avoid political and historical despair.

We do not simply experience frustration in searching for community. We come face-to-face with our finitude, our mortality, and our radical imperfection. The unattainability of community brings a realization of the circumstances most oppressive in our fate—that we exist in space and time, that we pass away like all other spatial and temporal realities, and that we are not even approximately what we could be and should be.

And not only is guilt uncovered in our quest for community; guilt is incurred. The effort to establish community is not innocuous. On the contrary, it tempts us into betraying, both in action and in thought, the ideal of community itself. And since man is a communal being, man himself is thus betrayed. Uncompromising communality draws us, paradoxically, into attitudes that are tyrannous and callous—into extremes of anticommunality.

Neither by renunciation nor by action can we escape from this situation. We cannot renounce the ideal of community altogether because that would be to renounce ourselves and our essential concerns. On the other hand, we cannot by being more prudent or more determined bring community into being because the obstacles to community are not of a kind that yield to action, and community is not a possible object of action.

The picture we are contemplating is not one of unrelieved desolation. Communal relationships of a fragmentary and ephemeral kind are possible. Otherwise, friendship and fidelity would not exist; and constitutionalism and democracy, which make possible a degree of community, would not be morally preferable to despotism. Our lives would lack all significance. As it is, our situation is not as bad as all of that. Yet it is worse by a great deal than enthusiasts of community typically take into account.

Some of the most excruciating of contemporary experiences may be attributed to the lure and unattainability of community. Both Russian and Chinese despotism are based on a philosophy calling for total communal integration; fascism was a hysterical flight from personal isolation into neotribal totalitarianism. Even America, spared some of the worst of Europe's terrors, has experienced the contradiction between man's communal nature and his alienated condition. This is expressed in phrases like "the lonely crowd" and "the organization man"—phrases representing, on the part of an individualistic people habituated to personal solitude, a discovery of the depths and torments of alienation.

Then how is political despair to be avoided? Why not withdraw from society and the public world, freeing one's life so far as possible from pain, as advocated by Epicurus in another discouraging time? Or why not, like fascists of a generation ago, throw ourselves into action that may in the long run be futile but is in the short run exhilarating and fulfilling? Why, in short, should we be civil?

The Failure of Ideology

No satisfactory answer can be found in the established ideologies. The tragic contradiction between our nature and condition cannot be understood and borne by following the typical counsels of radicalism, conservatism, or liberalism. Let us see why this is so.

As for radicalism the reason is rather clear. The crux of radicalism is communal urgency—a determination that community shall here and now come into being. The preceding reflections suggest that such urgency is inappropriate and dangerous. The most benign and relentless will, even the most intelligent will, cannot create a community. True, one can imagine a religious radicalism, demanding immediate community, recognizing the demand as contrary to any rational appraisal of reality, and leaving to God the resolution of the contradiction. Simone Weil exemplifies a radicalism such as this—in her political life far to the left, in her personal life a Christian mystic who seemingly counted little on historical change. A position of this kind is distant from normal radicalism, however, and it is doubtful whether it is logically coherent.

Conservatism (in its European form as distinguished from its American form, which is really a species of liberalism) is scarcely less communal than is radicalism. It disagrees with radicalism primarily with respect to means; community depends on tradition and rank, and it is not to be attained by sudden change but only by patient care for established institutions and by cautious reform. But community then is not a tragic ideal. On the contrary it is quite attainable; to reach it we need only to be prudent and humble. The pessimism and sense of limits often ascribed to conservatism are only relative. Moderate hope, not tragedy, is the keynote of the conservative consciousness.

Radicalism and conservatism, then, both manifest communal optimism. Both see man's essence and condition as fundamentally harmonious. Liberalism is different. Liberals traditionally grant the existence of irresolvable tensions between the individual and society. Their political and social views can be understood as products of an effort to come to terms with these tensions—to find ways of living well in spite of them. The basis on which liberals accommodate themselves to man's alienated condition, however, is a denial of his communal essence. In liberal ideology of the traditional sort there is little concern for community. Certain liberal thinkers have tried to introduce such a concern, but they have been in conscious opposition to an individualism that is of long standing, and remains an essential element, in the liberal outlook. Hence it is not in assuming the historical possibility of community that liberalism fails, but rather in neglecting the power and depth of the communal drive. Radicalism and conservatism misconstrue man's condition, liberalism his essence. In all instances alike the tragic character of the communal ideal is lost from sight.

Objections might be raised in behalf of any of these ideologies. For example, must not civility involve the radical habit of stubbornly opposing every injustice? Must it not embrace the conservative willingness to endure what cannot be immediately improved? And surely, in the face of the tragic inaccessibility of community, civility means liberality—limiting the power of government and society, resisting the communal pretensions of all institutions.

All of this may be admitted, even emphasized. The fault of the ideologies is not that they are wholly untrue, but that they typically claim to be wholly true. An ideology is a political theory serving as a guide to life and action for large numbers of people; that status is not won by showing that life is tragic or internally contradictory. In consequence, reigning ideologies treat community either as attainable or as not particularly desirable.

Acknowledging that community is a tragic ideal involves a strain. It means living within circumstances far different from the simple and hopeful situations outlined in the prevailing political creeds. Consciously bearing this strain is the heart of civility. It should not be inferred that civility is only for the precious few who hold themselves above the simple-mindedness of the masses. Indeed, ordinary people are probably less susceptible to the charms of the ideologies than are members of intellectual elites. What is essential is to transcend—as ordinary people, through commonsense skepticism, often do—the deceptively simple and lustrous alternatives commonly appealed to in public discourse.

If an adequate understanding of civility cannot be gained from any of the established ideologies, however, where should one look?

The Nature of Civility

Here we can only note, without following, certain pathways for reflection, and we can note no more than a few of those that are available. In doing this, it may be helpful to recall a well-known theory of Sören Kierkegaard's—a theory holding that there are three main stages of life, the aesthetic, the ethical, and the religious.[3] An aesthetic life, for Kierkegaard, was one devoted not necessarily to the enjoyment of art, but to worldly gratification of some kind—to physical pleasure, artistic delight, or perhaps the enjoyment of power. Living aesthetically, one dwells within the moment. Living ethically repre-

3. These are systematically outlined in Regis Jolivet, *Introduction to Kierkegaard*, trans. W. H. Barber (New York: E. P. Dutton, 1946), 110–201.

sents a fundamentally different personal orientation. Decisions are made not according to prospects of worldly gratification but according to the moral law, and hence, rather than dwelling in the moment, one dwells in an eternal order. As for the religious stage of life, through faith man transcends both the aesthetic and the ethical stages. Living by faith, one must be prepared not only to forego worldly satisfaction but even to break the moral law, as was Abraham when he made ready to murder Isaac in obedience to the command of God.

How can this schema be applied to the problem of remaining civil before the tragic limitations surrounding us? The answer is (and at this point we branch off from Kierkegaard, who had little interest in politics) that it enables us to conceive of three types of civility, each providing a possible way of confronting the dangers inherent in the communal ideal. I shall sketch these briefly.

AESTHETIC CIVILITY. In this stance one is sustained by the pleasures of power and participation. Aesthetic civility is exemplified by Niccolò Machiavelli. This does not mean that aesthetic civility is beyond all morality. The portrait of Machiavelli as a cynic (Shakespeare's "murderous Machiavel") is overdrawn. He was not indifferent to moral considerations or political decencies. In Machiavelli's mind, however, a political life is not justified primarily by the opportunities it provides for moral action. It is justified by the joys of power.

Thus is tragedy made tolerable. A practitioner of aesthetic civility might recognize the value of community; his political actions might express his own communal inclinations—by being planned and accomplished, for example, with respectful regard for the opinions of critics. Thus his enjoyment of power would not necessarily be either callous or uncomplicated. That enjoyment, nevertheless, would be the major motive underlying his political vocation. Would it be amiss to see an example of aesthetic civility in the presidency of John F. Kennedy?

ETHICAL CIVILITY. An ethical person is not upset fundamentally—not at the very foundations of his being—by tragedy. The one thing that matters is fidelity to the right, and this can be maintained regardless of events. Even as the whole world is being destroyed, ethical civility might provide the tranquillity of an all-encompassing and enduring order.

Ethical civility has proven itself in history. In some of the worst of times under Rome, the Stoics called on men to transcend the troubled cities in which they lived and enter into a cosmic and eternal city, a city ruled by laws that each one could read in his own conscience and mind. Stoicism not only strengthened individuals in their personal lives; it helped uphold them in their public lives during times when history offered little hope. A moving expression of ethical civility can be found in the *Meditations* of Marcus Aurelius.

RELIGIOUS CIVILITY. Christianity in ancient times was not markedly civil. The earliest Christians held aloof from political life; later, after the Church gained recognition and power, they drowned civility in religious intolerance. But Christianity contains richer sources of civility than this record suggests. What is decisive, perhaps, is that community is affirmed (in the standard of love) but indefinitely postponed; it becomes the anticipated climax, and end, of history. In leading to such a climax, history is meaningful and calls for human participation. Yet, since the conflict between the human essence and the human condition is historically unresolvable, participants are freed from the demand that strains civility so acutely, the demand for perfect community here and now.

Standing on the ground of religious civility, one may look on tragic times with a resignation outwardly stoic; in looking toward the ultimate future, however, one envisages a community far more living and concrete than the universal order inspiring the ethical mind. Hence resignation is only provisional. Christian civility is the outward form of a limitless hope.

Today, our task is not simple. We must take care not to forget that our ultimate concern is community—since we thus would forget our very humanity—but not to suppose that with resolution and effort community can be ours. The task, strictly speaking, is quixotic. Cervantes' knight was faithful to an unattainable ideal, yet fundamentally equable and harmless.

But the task offers little room for sentimentality. Self-pitying tears for "the impossible dream" do not answer to the contradictory demands of our situation. If our inmost being calls for community, while inalterable conditions deny us community, our need is for strength and sobriety. This is indicated by the three types of civility. Each one prescribes a solitary and difficult life—a life of political activity without ultimate hope, a life of dispassionate rectitude, and a life of adherence to an ideal deferred to the end of historical time. Is man capable of disciplines so onerous? Only if we answer that he is not will the worst—for all of the evils of the past—have befallen us, for then we shall have accepted despair.

II / ON THE NATURE OF COMMUNITY

   A serious difficulty lies at the core of the prevailing view of community. It is assumed that a community is simply a highly cohesive unit of society, such as an old ethnic neighborhood or a small, isolated town. Any distinction between community and society is put in terms of *Gemeinschaft* and *Gesellschaft*, and community accordingly is understood as the spontaneous and impassioned unity of, say, a primitive tribe in contrast with the calculated unity of a modern factory.[1] The yearning for community is presumably for a life organically and unreflectively bound together with the lives of others.

  Yet the word "community" tacitly says, "Here human beings are truly united." It proclaims not mere unity but unity based on recognition of the essential being of all participants. Hence the idea of community, taken seriously, engenders suspicion of what are often called "communities," for these, as many who have fled the neighborhood or town in which they were born well know, often discourage essential human qualities—rationality, freedom, creativity. In a word, "communities" do not seem very communal.

  The problem is not merely one of theoretical incoherence. If a community is only a highly cohesive unit of society, yet fulfills the deepest human desires, then the more unity the better. The ideal of community becomes that of a social and political monolith. Moreover, mere social unity is a possible object of action. It thus becomes reasonable to think that man may forcibly create the monolith that is community and should, from fidelity to humanity, try his utmost to do

---

 1. See Ferdinand Tönnies, *Community and Society*, trans. Charles P. Loomis (New York: Harper & Row, 1957).

so. Qualities such as rationality and freedom become threatening— threatening, ironically, to the goal of uniting human beings in their essence.

Human beings are unsettled and searching creatures. If community unites them as they are in their essential being, it must be quite different from a tribe, from an artifact of revolutionary despotism, and from anything else we can readily point to in the world around us. It must be more impermanent, personal, and elusive. It must be a reality partaking of movement and freedom.

How can community be conceived of in this way? What concept of unity can take full account of man's unsettled and searching nature? The reflections recorded in the following pages center on this question.

Breaking with the old idea of community is not easy, however. We must not only contend with habit—that of equating community and unified society. We must also deal with difficulties involved in thinking of community as something that cannot be equated with any fixed and observable reality—difficulties involved in conceptualizing something essentially personal and free. In order to help in disentangling ourselves from older and easier habits of thought I suggest that we try out a concept unassociated, in many minds, with community: the concept of inquiry.

I base this suggestion on the idea that man is essentially an inquirer. A human being transcends every social role in which he finds himself, and he does this by questioning and criticizing—by raising doubts concerning the role itself and concerning society as a whole. He does this not only because of the enduring inadequacies of society but also because he is a being in search of being, his own being and that of others. One searches through social criticism and political controversy; one searches through science and art, through philosophy and religion; one searches in daily life and conversation. To search in these ways is to inquire, and to do this by virtue of one's nature is to show that one is essentially an inquirer. The implications for community are easily seen: if community unites people in their essential being, community must be in the nature of inquiry.

It may seem that inquiry is too intellectual an activity for adequately characterizing community. But perhaps we interpret inquiry in too intellectual a fashion. It might be argued that every truly human activity should be carried out in a thoughtful and searching—an inquiring—manner and that only thus is experience fully appropriated by a being possessing the faculty of reason.

It may seem that inquiry is essentially solitary. But perhaps our understanding of inquiry has been distorted not only by a false intellectualism but also by a false individualism. If I inquire, must I not inquire of others? And if I inquire in solitude must I not find imaginary interlocutors in my own mind, thus creating an inner dialogue?

Inquiry is nothing but serious communication, and it may be that understanding community depends above all on rejoining two concepts that have become strangely dissociated in our thinking—community and communication.

In trying to work out and examine these hypotheses we shall begin by considering the consciousness of the estranged individual. That is, we shall consider consciousness that is problematic, that consequently does not unite its possessor with reality or with other minds, and that gives rise to inquiry. This is to begin analytically, so to speak, where we begin existentially. Thus a basis will be laid for understanding inquiry and communication.

First, I shall suggest a rough interpretation of the structure of consciousness. Limits of space will force me to simplify drastically. This can be justified, I hope, by the fact that what I shall sketch is not a new theory of consciousness but only a version of the view set forth by Immanuel Kant and by certain contemporary followers of Kant, above all Karl Jaspers and Nicolas Berdyaev.[2]

The Fragmentation of Consciousness

We are conscious in several different ways, and the same reality is often apprehended through two or more different modes of consciousness. The discontinuities of consciousness are only temporarily and precariously overcome. We thus are habituated to them and during our daily lives more or less automatically suppress and coordinate the various modes of consciousness in order to inhabit a unified world. But as

2. See Karl Jaspers, *Philosophy*, trans. E. B. Ashton (3 vols.; Chicago: University of Chicago Press, 1969). Among Berdyaev's many works, *The Beginning and the End*, trans. R. M. French (London: Geoffrey Bles, 1952), probably contains the most uncompromising statement of his Kantian position.

soon as we set aside the practical problems of everyday life and try to gain a sure and thorough knowledge of reality as a whole or of any reality in particular we realize that we lack an integral apprehension of being.

Following leads in the writings of the philosophers cited above, we may analyze consciousness in terms of four primary modes. Only two of these, which may be called "experience" and "awareness," are cognitive. They are not necessarily veridical, for their disclosures may be misconstrued; but we cannot dismiss them as illusory.

1. EXPERIENCE. The reality disclosed in experience is "the world" —the realm of things located in space and time, appearing through the senses, and readily fitting into rational categories such as quantity and causality. Experience thoroughly organized by reason is knowledge, certain and universal. Common sense largely equates experience and consciousness and assumes that reality in itself is that which is contained in experience. Common sense of this kind is supported by empiricism as a philosophical persuasion. The sole valid source of knowledge, for empiricists, is experience. For many, such a view is self-evident. In the history of philosophical speculation, however, it has been frequently and formidably challenged.

Experience according to Kant receives its structure altogether from the mind, and things as we experience them are therefore not the same as they are in themselves. Moreover, experience is not our only means of contact with things as they are in themselves. Perhaps Kant exaggerates the power of the mind in shaping experience. But the limitations of experience are indicated by the fact that reality does become indubitably present to us in another way.

2. AWARENESS. To say that I am "aware" of a reality usually means that I am conscious *that* it is but not necessarily of *what* it is. The content of awareness is existence—*that* things are. The content of knowledge is essence, or *what* things are. Thus awareness does not present different realities than does experience, and it is not quite accurate even to say that it tells us more about the realities within our experience. At its unchallengeable core it is only the consciousness that reality in itself is not the same as reality in our experience.

This may be clarified by noting three basic kinds of awareness. (1) One of these is subjectivity. We are aware, in every experience, of a self that has the experience but is not included within it. We are aware in knowing of a self that knows but is not wholly known. We do not thus learn anything *about* the self except that it is, and is not in its entirety an object of experience. (2) We are also aware in every experience of beings other than ourselves that are not the same in themselves as they are in our experience of them. Even a particular rock is not reducible altogether to that which I see before me as a rock. I realize this in apprehending it as this rock in particular, not the universal rock of organized experience. If a rock is not wholly comprised in experience, a human being who is loved is scarcely more than hinted at in experience. (3) The sense of a reality beyond experience is inherent not only in our consciousness of particular entities but also in our consciousness of the world as a whole. Each person's world is in some ways unique, and there is no such thing as an objective and all-inclusive world. Kant showed that such an entity cannot be conceived of without contradiction. "The world" is a way of organizing experience. Therefore, just as a thing-in-itself underlies everything we experience, so being-in-itself underlies every world.[3]

Every experience thus involves a penumbra of awareness. But awareness is probably sharpest in feelings such as guilt and love, in which I myself or another stand forth emphatically and mysteriously from the world and its objects. It may seem that awareness must concern only a small portion of reality. Such an impression, however, has no validity. It employs an experiential measure, that of quantity, thus presupposing the absolute character of a mode of consciousness that is relativized by awareness.

Phenomenology and existentialism stem from taking awareness seriously and consist primarily in elucidation of awareness. The richness of some phenomenological and existential philosophies shows how far awareness is from being merely marginal.

The other two modes of consciousness, typically represented by the artist and the saint, are dubitable. It is perhaps misleading to say this, for they are often personally overwhelming and have shaped human history. But their purported disclosures are not wholly in agreement nor

---

3. This aspect of awareness is elucidated by Karl Jaspers in *Reason and Existenz*, trans. William Earle (Noonday Press, 1955). See also Charles F. Wallraff, *Karl Jaspers: An Introduction to His Philosophy* (Princeton: Princeton University Press, 1970).

universally compelling, and we are not forced, as we are by disclosures of experience (such as an approaching automobile on a street one is about to cross), to believe them. The consciousness typified by the artist may be called "vision," that typified by the saint, "faith."

3. VISION. The average person probably partakes of vision most readily through the arts. A Rembrandt painting or a Mozart symphony seems to provide a different view of reality, at least momentarily, than we gain through experience or awareness. What is the difference? The sense of relief brought by great art seems to consist in a consciousness, illusory or not, of ultimate harmonies in which all reality is somehow redeemed. A single entity, such as a vase, may be an object both of experience and of vision. In ordinary experience, however, the vase is merely a thing that may be used, ignored, or discarded. In a painting by Van Gogh, however, it resolves tensions in a way that renders it a kind of benediction on all reality. Beauty possesses the mysterious power of seeming to justify neutral, or even unjustifiable, reality. It is perhaps in music and in tragic drama that this power is at its most imperious. What is its source?

Here reflection must become highly conjectural. But I suggest that vision provides an intuition—or illusion—of something experience clearly and consistently denies, that is, immortality. The sense that every person and every reality, even the earth itself, is fated for total extinction, threatens to deprive existence of all meaning. If all things and even all memories are at last to be totally erased, then what can really matter except for momentary pleasure? "Let us eat and drink," as Paul said, "for tomorrow we die."[4] Vision lifts the pall of mortality. It does not do this by speaking literally of immortality. It provides only intimations; but these can be so powerful, as in a Beethoven symphony or a Shakespearean tragedy, that even skeptics fall under their spell.

Vision is not confined to art, however. Most of the great philosophies, for example, have embodied an intuition of some everlasting reality—the Idea of the Good, natural law, the *élan vital*. Even certain atheists seem in their lives and writings to have been inspired by some symbol of eternity—Friedrich Nietzsche, for example, with his concept of "eternal recurrence," and Marx, prophet of an ultimate world-transformation. Political action, too, sometimes introduces into

4. I Corinthians 15:32

passing events intimations of something lasting. Ancient Romans envisioned the Empire as eternal; Americans have often seen themselves as servants of a universally and enduringly significant unfoldment of human powers. Finally, vision is as clearly manifest as it is anywhere in the moral life. Preeminent morality, especially when realized in acts of self-sacrifice, seems to express an apprehension of things more important than life and thus undefeated by death.

But should credence be given these hints of eternity? The answer lies in the fourth mode of consciousness.

4. FAITH. Through faith people feel not merely that they discern meaning and immortality but that they are in touch with the ultimate source of these qualities. If vision is of being, faith concerns the ground of being. Vision is only implicitly religious; faith is explicitly so.

William James wrote of "the will to believe." Such a will, however, is powerless. It is well-known that people sometimes wish to have faith, yet feel they cannot. It must be said, consequently, that faith is a gift. For those to whom it is given, the source of faith is necessarily thought of as God. Hence faith, in the minds of its possessors, is a response to revelation.

Whereas vision can be interpreted as a consciousness we gain through abilities and efforts of our own, the very concept of revelation implies initiative from the side of the revealed reality. For some people, art and philosophy are revelatory, but for most people faith comes in response to reports of revelation that are hallowed as scripture.

For many today, faith consists in dreams and delusions. How can faith claim authority alongside of science? It cannot, where faith and experience clash. Those speaking for faith blunder disastrously when they allow themselves to contest factual matters with trustworthy interpreters of experience. In its own sphere, however, which concerns the ground of things rather than the character of things as they are experienced, faith is invulnerable. Moreover, its power to shape human life is greater than that of any other mode of consciousness. Although uniquely dubitable, it is also uniquely compelling.

In sum, we look out on reality through four different apertures, as it were. We seem to see the same universe through all of them, yet in such a way that interpreting the character of that universe is difficult.

To speak less metaphorically, the four modes of consciousness do not constitute a mental structure that all must acknowledge. Contents of the dubitable modes of consciousness may be taken as disclosures of ultimate truth or as mere illusions. Every mode of consciousness can be interpreted and related to other modes of consciousness in various ways. Hence the overall structure of consciousness faces each person and each society as a question, not as an established state of affairs. In the Middle Ages, the ruling mode of consciousness was faith. In our own time, it is experience. The ultimate authority of experience is sanctioned by positivism and seems to many to be self-evident. But the principle that all truth is experiential is not itself experiential, and the positivistic organization of consciousness must thus be seen as merely allowed, and not required, by the intrinsic character of consciousness.

Cannot reason discover the true order of consciousness? It can certainly help in clarifying and relating the modes of consciousness. The whole body of science, for example, is a vast elucidation of experience, and theology constitutes a clarification of faith. Philosophy is a rational examination of consciousness as a whole and of the authority and inter-relationships of its modes. But reason could discover the *true* order of consciousness only if it could rationally establish the truth of its ultimate standard of truth. This of course would be to reason in a circle. Hence reason can only expose factual errors and logical inconsistencies but cannot arbitrate among competing interpretations of being as a whole. Philosophy, unlike science, reaches no decisive results; in our time, as in Plato's, there are numerous different philosophies to which a reasonable person may adhere.

From this view of consciousness it follows that we are naturally estranged. We have no assured and unified consciousness of being. We apprehend our fellow human beings, and all other beings as well, through discordant lenses. Is the person before me, as experience seems to say, a psychological mechanism that can be wholly understood through science? Is he, as awareness suggests, a presence transcending all that can be observed and measured, approachable only as a "Thou" rather than an "It," or perhaps not approachable at all? Should I try to understand him in the light of vision—perhaps as potentially the ideal figure disclosed in statues of antiquity? Or is the person I face one who has, as held in the Christian faith, been addressed and offered redemption by the Creator and Lord of all being?

Estrangement is painful and we try continually to overcome it. That is, we inquire. It is the very nature of our consciousness that makes us inquirers.

The Concept of Inquiry

Inquiry is simply the effort to elucidate and harmonize the modes of consciousness. It is the effort to enter by this means into the presence of being itself. The integration of consciousness would dissipate all doubt and spell the end of estrangement. Inquiry aims at overcoming the fragmentation of consciousness without illegitimately distorting or suppressing any of its modes.

We inquire, however, in two different ways. We inquire *about*, and we inquire *with*; we inquire *about* various objects of inquiry, and we inquire *with* fellow inquirers. In the former way we seek theoretical or aesthetic contemplation; in the latter way community. Both are efforts to harmonize the modes of consciousness and overcome estrangement. Through one, however, the individual strives to integrate consciousness through solitary effort, whereas through the other a cooperative effort occurs. Consequently, we may refer to one as individualistic inquiry and to the other as dialogical inquiry. The latter, as we shall see, is in itself community.

We shall begin by considering individualistic inquiry. Or rather, we shall begin by considering inquiry *as though* it were individualistic. If the aims of inquiry are to be fulfilled, individualistic and dialogical inquiry must be joined; consciousness can be unified only through dialogue. Solitary and dialogical effort, reflection and communication, are merely aspects of a single activity.

In actuality, we persistently try to carry on this activity in a purely individualistic manner. This stems from a desire to avoid the humbling and dependent status implicit in dialogical inquiry. In pride, I try to master reality through my own independent mind. Only by overcoming pride, usually in response to necessities arising in the course of inquiry, do I recognize the inescapably dialogical character of inquiry— and thus prepare for entry into community. Here again, then, analytical order—considering inquiry first as though it were purely individual-istic—corresponds with existential order.

What justifies the analytical order is that dialogical inquiry not only arises from individualistic inquiry but must retain an individualistic core: a sense of intellectual independence and responsibility on the part of each inquirer. Hence, to consider inquiry as though it were indi-vidualistic, and then to take account of the conditions that compel it to be dialogical, is an analytical convenience that does not distort the sub-ject under examination.

The basic types of inquiry can be understood on the basis of, al-though not in strict correspondence with, the modes of consciousness.

1. SCIENTIFIC INQUIRY. Science is concerned with the invariable order implicit in experience. Hence it is directed toward relationships that are universal and are not identical with empirical relationships. Yet theories that have not been empirically validated, and are not implied by theories that have been, are unacceptable.

2. HISTORICAL INQUIRY. Comprising not only history but also much that is presented as social science, historical inquiry is concerned with the actual order of experience. Its field is defined by experience and awareness together and thus includes not only all that falls within or-ganized experience but also the particularities—the persons, the places, the events—that are not wholly reducible to universals.

3. TRANSCENDENTAL INQUIRY. Picasso once said, "I never do a painting as a work of art. All of them are researches. I search constantly and there is a logical sequence in all this research."[5] This shows that inquiry can be carried on through art. Theological writing shows that it can be carried on through religion. Artistic and religious inquiry is tran-scendental in the sense of being concerned not with the world and its objects but with the ultimate being that transcends the world. Whereas scientific inquiry deals primarily with experience, transcendental in-quiry relies on vision and faith. The order of experience is subordinated to the disclosure of meaning and is often freely altered for this purpose, as in fiction and in myth.

4. PHILOSOPHICAL INQUIRY. The comprehensive mode of inquiry is philosophy. The comprehensiveness of philosophy is not the same as

5. Quoted in Alexander Liberman, *The Artist in His Studio* (New York: Viking Press, 1960), 112.

sovereignty. Apart from scientific, historical, and transcendental inquiry, philosophy is empty. It has the unique function, nevertheless, of uniting all modes of consciousness in a single interpretation of being. Whereas other forms of inquiry depend on particular modes of consciousness, philosophical inquiry has its own unique foundation in reason—the supreme faculty, as Kant defines it, for reaching "the highest unity of thought."[6]

To say that inquiry may take the form of science, history, art, religion, or philosophy, is not to imply that these always, or even often, take the form of inquiry. Men again and again treat their conceptions as final and unquestionable. They do this in every form of inquiry. Scientific theories are made into changeless, all-inclusive views of being, as in the materialistic philosophy of Thomas Hobbes; history is conceived of as a total and inevitable order of events; cultural styles are frozen into orthodox aesthetic standards, as when supporters of academic painting in nineteenth-century France tried to suppress impressionism; religious faith is degraded into an objective explanation of the origin of the species; philosophy falls away from its classical definition as the *love* of wisdom and claims conclusive knowledge. In all of these ways inquiry is abandoned.

When this happens, however, I suggest that humanity itself is abandoned because it is of the human essence to ask after, but not to possess, the truth. Man is always, as Jaspers says, more than he knows about himself. Every definition that equates man with a fixed set of rationally comprehensible traits is necessarily false. A particular mode of consciousness and a particular interpretation of its disclosures are taken as unquestionable. But the being who is supposedly encased in that definition—man himself—can invoke other modes of consciousness and other conceptions of reality. The questioning in itself is a sign of the inadequacy of the definition.

The principle that man is an inquirer implies not only that he *can* but also that he *must* inquire. Man is a being oriented toward being: this is an idea recurrent in philosophy from a time earlier than Socrates to the present. It is confirmed by traditional values. Beauty provides a feeling

6. This concept of reason is developed in the "Transcendental Dialectic" in *The Critique of Pure Reason*, trans. Norman Kemp Smith (London: Macmillan & Co., 1958), 297–570. The quotation is to be found on p. 300.

of the full, sensual presence of being; truth is its intellectual presence; most moral rules are commanded by respect for being; and the principal misdeeds—murder, robbery, deceit—are denials of being. And is not all fear, as of disease and death, fear of the loss of being? Freud at times saw the "death wish," an urge to destruction, as permanent and primal. But introspection, and consideration of nihilistic political regimes like Hitler's, suggest a less pessimistic hypothesis: that destructive inclinations arise from despair and that annihilation becomes an end in itself only for those who find a more basic impulse, that toward the realization of being, everywhere blocked and defeated. Nor can this impulse be reduced to the instinct of self-preservation, for it is not merely one's own being that is prized. To live securely, but everlastingly alone, as on a deserted planet, is no one's dream of life.

Someone may object that contact with being is not found in inquiry itself but only in the conclusions of inquiry. This would be so, however, only were we able to transcend being, objectifying it in changeless theories. What we call "matters of fact"—the year Julius Caesar was killed, the composition of water—can thus be objectified. But the supposition that man and all reality can be comes from thinking of consciousness as though it were nothing but experience. Being itself is conceived of as totally accessible to observation and theoretical comprehension. The only way to avoid such illusions is to subject every "complete and final truth" to inquiry, thus maintaining the principle that truth lies in inquiry as a whole, not in its results alone.

One possible objection—that the idea of man as essentially an inquirer is too intellectualist an interpretation—was referred to earlier. It is true that inquiry presupposes involvement of the intellect. It does not follow, however, that inquiry is carried on only in libraries and seminar rooms. To recall the best accounts of farming, sexual love, sports, and other nonintellectual activities is to realize how large a part in those activities is played by trial, reflection, and other elements of inquiry. Indeed, it may be an inquiring attitude, and an underlying reverence for being, that saves activities of this kind from debasement by greed, lust, and other destructive passions.

Intellectualism is precluded wherever care is taken that inquiry is not stifled by its own conclusions. As an ideal of rational elucidation, the concept of inquiry expresses trust in the intellect; but as an ideal of elucidation that never ceases, it rules out the idolatry of intellect that substitutes theory for being.

The paradoxical nature of inquiry—that the truth is found in the search itself—is manifest in the life and dialogues of Socrates. The dialogues that presumably describe most accurately the conversations of Socrates himself end inconclusively. Socrates' whole life of dialogue, moreover, ends inconclusively, for in the trial that led to his death Socrates claimed no wisdom except that inherent in the consciousness of his own ignorance. Yet he had devoted his life to inquiry, and his composure in approaching death—devoting his last hours to an inconclusive discussion of the immortality of the soul—showed that he was ignorant only in the sense that what he knew could not be embodied in theoretical conclusions.

Beyond exemplifying the paradoxical nature of inquiry, the figure of Socrates suggests why it is possible to say that man is an inquirer. Plato's picture of Socrates is of one engaged, simply and unaffectedly, yet with complete singleness of mind, in a lifetime of inquiry. He informed the jury that he would return, if released, to the kind of questioning that had led to his arrest. Sentenced to die, he pursued his efforts at clarifying consciousness until a few minutes before the end. Nothing whatever could deflect him from his ironic and imperturbable pursuit of truth.

One other quality of Socrates must attract our attention—one that brings us to the subject of dialogical, as distinguished from individualistic, inquiry. Although rejected by all but a handful of friends, Socrates always sought the truth by talking with others. He was indefeasibly communal.

Community as Inquiry

I inquire with others because I must. I discover that individualistic inquiry cannot deal with a disturbing kind of awareness—an awareness of strange minds, of minds that are not only unknown and unpredictable but that have the unsettling power of casting into doubt the order established in my own mind. We are such inveterate objectifiers that we have to guard against trying to unify consciousness by treating everything that enters into it as simply an object of experience. Doing this, we envision inquiry as solitary and truth as the possession of a single mind.

But thus we falsify our consciousness. In awareness, we are conscious of realities that cannot be wholly objectified—of the self, for example, and of other selves. Consciousness therefore cannot be unified through systematic objectification. It can be unified only through harmonious intersubjectivity, through sharing and cooperatively questioning all interpretations of the contents of consciousness.

It may be asked at what stage in the process of inquiry do others enter in. When does the inquirer come under the necessity of leaving the sphere of his own mind in order to inquire in common with other minds? At the very outset, I suggest. Granted, this may not be recognized. The inquirer may persist indefinitely in the proud effort to master reality alone, without engaging in the humble act of consulting others. It is an illusion, however, to think that even organizing experience is a solitary activity. The simplest objective observation—taking note, for example, of the weather—is implicitly communal, for the concept of objectivity is equivalent to that of absolutely reliable intersubjectivity. To suppose that valid inquiry is solitary in its initial, or objective, stages, and that it is necessarily communal only in other stages, is tacitly to accept an individualistic premise that is bound to inhibit understanding of the full identity of inquiry and community.

Others are present in the very state of estrangement that inquiry presupposes. It is not merely that human beings are peculiarly difficult to fit into any integrated scheme of consciousness. It is also that they disturb whatever scheme one person devises by propounding differing schemes of their own. They are sources, not merely objects, of inquiry. Perhaps I am trying to understand human beings as psychological mechanisms. But I find not only that they are not as reliable as mechanisms should be, but that some of them understand human beings in a different way, perhaps as creatures of God. Others in these ways threaten my efforts at clarification; both by their behavior and their words they tend to keep me trammeled by the uncertainties and confusions of a divided mind. I may of course try to ignore them, even to suppress them. But that is to strive for unity of consciousness through will and power rather than through reason. Persons who stand outside our interpretations, inexplicable and challenging, yet ignored or suppressed, are signs that the process of inquiry is incomplete and that we fear the venture of trying to complete it.

The discovery of our plurality comes about in a variety of ways. One way, for example, is through the disturbing realization that I am seen by someone else as a completely different sort of person than I think of myself as being; this realization comes in a particularly jarring form if I am attacked, physically or even verbally. We also discover our plurality simply when we differ in our interpretations of the realities about us. A field that for one person is a source of beauty is for another person a favorable commercial site; the plurality of minds is manifest. But I find other minds even in myself. The successive and incongruous states of my own consciousness, and the effort to harmonize them through inquiry, place me in a situation analagous to that created by a plurality of minds.

However it comes about, the discovery of plurality imposes the necessity of inquiring not only about, but with, other persons. Each one properly tries to formulate a unified interpretation of the contents of consciousness. But never does an interpretation become complete and unquestionable except by delusions and violence. The most valid interpretations are those that incorporate in themselves, like Platonic dialogues, recognition that they are fragmentary and tentative and take on truth only in a dialogical setting that denies them finality.

To encounter other persons is to encounter beings whom I can address and to whom I can offer attention. They are beings who can share and confirm explanations I devise, or can dispute and sometimes destroy such explanations, but cannot themselves be altogether explained. This is why the unification of consciousness must come about not simply through individual reasoning but through dialogical reasoning.

It is why the ideal of unified consciousness is an ideal of community. In discovering that man is an inquirer, we discover simultaneously that he is a communal being, a seeker of truth that is fully shared. More precisely, he is a seeker of truth that is *universally* shared. Just as a tyrant, trying to unify consciousness through violence, cannot tolerate a single dissenting voice, so man in his communal integrity, trying to unify consciousness through inquiry, cannot ignore a single questioning mind.

Inquiry, then, takes place through communication and in that way alone. In this sense, inquiry is community. Having reached this conclusion, we can move a step further by reversing the proposition and asserting that community is inquiry. The familiar idea that community consists in agreement of any kind, that it consists, for example, in common acceptance of a narrow and stifling set of customs inherited from the past, or in widespread acceptance of an advertising message, grossly distorts human nature and obscures the ideal of community. It tends to reconcile human beings to social conditions under which they are far less than they should be and are estranged from one another even though they may be totally united through whatever forms of truncated selfhood they have accepted. Community can live only if people insist again and again, by speech and occasionally by violent resistance, that not any kind of unity that habit, circumstances, or a momentary elite can induce everyone to accept is a community. Only cooperation in the most serious human concerns—and this means above all in the exploration of being—calls forth a community. It is moving testimony to the nature, as well as the value, of community when dissidents in a totalitarian regime risk their freedom and lives to speak in defiance of the monolithic social and political unity that such regimes create. A solitary voice, speaking with utmost seriousness, is a far more decisive sign of community than is a nation unified merely by force and propaganda, or by commercial convenience and advertising.

If community brings together human beings as they are in essence, then it is found in full measure only as we contend in common against the fragmentation of consciousness. Our one serious responsibility is that of understanding the truth as fully as possible and in that way becoming ourselves. We form a community only by being united in the acceptance of that responsibility. This is not a new theory, but rather the ancient premise of intellectual and artistic activity restated in opposition to the casual and destructive misuse of the communal ideal in recent times.

It will be clear by now why we must say that community is inquiry rather than the *result* of inquiry. It has already been suggested that truth is found in inquiry itself and not only at its end; to sever truth from the questions lying at its source is to objectify being and in this way to lose the truth. Community, presumably, lies in sharing the truth, and if this is so it must be inherent in the very process of searching for the truth.

The history of political thought reveals a strong tendency to think of community as realized only when the struggles of thought and history have been ended. Thus for Plato the kingship of philosophers was the center of an order superior to history; for Augustine, the City of God was established only with the end of all earthly events; in Marxism, capitalism prepares the way for communism economically but is meaningless spiritually and may as well be totally forgotten once communism is achieved. Of course we cannot simply assert the opposite, as though community were present in every moment of history. Should we not be wary, however, of too sharply separating the dangers and uncertainties of history from the communal finale for which we hope? Is there not sense of some kind in the Johannine idea that the end of history must be found and lived in the present moment? Community is surely a state of life; and if that is so, it must in some way partake of movement, doubt, and insecurity.

To look again at another objection noted earlier in these reflections, a critic might say that inquiry is not essentially communal and that this is apparent in the lives of some of the most courageous seekers after truth—people who have been neglected, even scorned and persecuted, by their contemporaries. Socrates exemplifies this criticism; at the same time, he suggests a response.

Socrates was scorned and finally killed, yet in his own personal bearing he was thoroughly communal. This indicates that an inquirer may, by speaking and listening even to those who are inattentive and silent, place himself in a communal setting—beyond false absolutes and in the presence of persons. He may thus stand in the sphere of truth. It seems that there is such a state as solitary communality and that one person alone may establish inquiring relationships by assuming a stance of attentiveness and availability. Perhaps inquiry is greatly handicapped where mutuality is lacking. But the integrity of the inquirer is not destroyed. Socrates was not less inquiring, nor less communal, because of the hostility of other Athenians.

The difference between community and social unity can now be clearly seen. True, community is entered into through communication, and communication depends on certain kinds of social unity, such as common language and similar values. But community is not equivalent to, is not assured by, and may come into conflict with, social unity. Man is shaped and confined by society, but not wholly. To a degree, he transcends society; he can use it, question it, change it, destroy it.

Community brings together persons in their essential being and therefore cannot consist in the social unity that persons partially transcend.

This implies a view of tradition. Society as an inheritance comes into our hands in the form of tradition. The communal ideal is that tradition be wholly absorbed in inquiry, that it be examined rationally, and that it be accepted, revised, or repudiated in complete clarity of mind. In other words, our communality entails an effort to master society as the collective past and to relate it, if only by consciously accepting it, to the living present. We can never succeed in doing this. We have no standpoint outside of tradition that would make it possible. To inquire into one aspect of tradition we must use standards and assumptions derived from other aspects of tradition. But there is nothing in tradition as such that is sacred or inviolable. There are sacred traditions but not things that are sacred because they are traditions. People joined by uncriticized traditions are not joined in community.

Community as inquiry often imperils social unity. Then society will be hostile to community. Just as the nature of community is visible in the life of Socrates, so the tragic antithesis of community and society is visible in the death of Socrates.

We are now in a favorable position for considering how much community should mean to us. Misunderstandings in this matter often arise from confusing community and society. Having clarified the distinction between them, perhaps we can avoid these misunderstandings.

The Value of Community

The ideal of community is a personalistic version of the oneness with being that is the supreme good if man is a being oriented toward being. It is an expression of the concept formulated in very different ways in the Upanishads, the dialogues of Plato, and the works of Augustine: that a state of ontological unity is the goal of human life.

Many criticisms ostensibly concerned with the value of community apply in reality only to society. Since society does not unite human beings in their essence it cannot be unconditionally good. Membership in any social group requires a weighing of gains and losses. Community, however, is not subject to similar calculations. A revolt against community is never justified, although community may require a revolt against society. Aristotle's objection that Plato sought excessive unity can be valid only in reference to society, for there cannot be excessive community. In practice, of course, no relationship is purely communal, and every actual relationship thus involves some loss. But the loss is in community.

It is often assumed that individuality and freedom are incompatible with community and may be chosen instead of community. But no one desires, or can realize, individuality and freedom in isolation. One achieves selfhood only for, and in the presence of, others. Thus, for example, one may seek individuality through artistic creativity or utilize his freedom in scholarly research. But these are communal activities; they make selfhood and freedom real through communication. A person is not a definite and finished being who desires community as he might desire a drink of water or a new garment or anything else that is merely added on to an already existent being. Entering into community is not linking a completed self with others; rather, it is forming the self in association with others. Hence, contrary to conventional views, the desire for community and the desire for individuality and freedom are ultimately the same. This is implied in interpreting man as an inquirer and community as inquiry.

If a human being were merely an object of experience, then community could be understood like any other combination of objects, such as a stone wall. But a human being, unlike an object of experience such as a stone, is not finished and wholly present in his empirical nature. He must be formed and discovered through the clarification of consciousness that takes place in inquiry or communication. A person is not weakened or destroyed by community, although he often is by society. If anything is weakened or destroyed by community, it is not the person. Rather, it is an objectification that may be accepted by the person as his real self but is, nevertheless, like wreckage on the sea, evidence that personal being has been lost.

Our admiration for people whose lives have been characterized by solitude, rebellion, or martyrdom—for those who have seemed more defiant than communal—does not necessarily express reservations about the value of community. The defiance we esteem is often not of community but of legal and social forms that inhibit community. Rousseau is an example. All of his life he was divided from others by his self-consciousness and his resentments. These qualities, however, were in some part responses to a society that left little room for community. And Rousseau's greatness lay in the eloquence and profundity of his refusal to acquiesce in his estrangement. He tried to understand the conditions under which life could be more communal, and through his writings he addressed his fellow humans, in this way doing all he could to establish communal relationships.

Nietzsche is another solitary figure who exemplifies man's fundamental communality. He does this in spite of himself, for he professed little concern for community. Nietzsche exalted creativity and was in his own life defiantly and uncompromisingly original. The creator, Nietzsche held, must regard with disdain, or ignore, most human beings. But why, according to Nietzsche, must the creator adopt such an attitude? Because most people cannot understand and appreciate true creativity. Is this not to say, however, that they are incapable of taking part in authentic communication? Creativity is essentially communal. A painter or writer does not destroy his works when they are finished but puts them before the world. As a philosopher of creativity, Nietzsche was concerned ultimately with community; as a writer, Nietzsche was engaged in communication and he wished desperately to be heard.

Creativity is often treated as highly individualistic, and it is, so far as the creative person refuses to do what is merely pleasing to others. He uncompromisingly expresses *himself*. But he *expresses* himself, he creates something that is to be seen or heard or read. His creativity evinces his communality.

Truth is sometimes thought of as a value imposing solitude or martyrdom on those devoted to it and thus as a value apart from community. But we can think of the truth only as that which all would recognize if they could see things with perfect clarity. Truth is that which links human beings when they rise above confusion and dishonesty, and in that way it is the substance of community. A bearer of the truth might be solitary or persecuted and yet, in his grasp of the truth, be in a certain sense at one with all humanity.

It may seem that there are values having little to do with community: exercising a skill, enjoying food and wine, even fighting, as shown in some accounts of battle.[7] But such values do not jeopardize the moral primacy of community so long as they can be shared, and shared in that searching and careful way that we mean when we speak of inquiry. Community arises when persons together realize their essential being. Hence any value is communal if it can engage the interest of man in his essence and can be subjected to continuing efforts at clarification. Many things human beings care about (as well as some things they do not care about) have indeterminate communal potentialities. The extent of those potentialities can only be discovered by trial and error, by inquiry. Some things human beings care about of course turn out, under communal examination, to engage our interest only when we are confused or inwardly divided; they turn out to be unsuitable as communal bonds. When that happens, however, we realize that they are not to be greatly valued or even must be condemned. Community, then, not only possesses value in itself but tests and sometimes enhances the value of things that are shared.

Equating community and inquiry implies no modification of the principle that community is a tragic ideal. Rather it confirms that principle, for inquiry too is tragic. We inquire haltingly and ineffectively; at best we discover only fragments of the truth and we are destined to end our lives in ignorance. But equating community and inquiry enables us to see not only why community is tragic but also why it is an ideal. Through inquiring communication we enter into being in its depth and mystery and we gain a sense of ourselves in our restless, reflective, and companionable essence.

7. On the values that may be found even in trench warfare, see Guy Chapman, *A Passionate Prodigality: Fragments of Autobiography* (Greenwich, Conn.: Fawcett Publications, 1967).

III / POLITICAL COMMUNITY

The very phrase, political community, is a contradiction in terms. It denotes an association sustained at once by power and by communication. This might lead one to think that communality entails anarchism—a complete rejection of politics. Our reflections already, however, have suggested a far different and more paradoxical idea: that through politics we experience and accept the tensions inherent in being human, those of living as communal beings in a universe that is unfavorable to community. We may approach this issue by establishing some broad distinctions.

Types of Community

It is an ancient and widespread assumption that the potential communality of any association is decisively affected by the numbers involved. Genuine community supposedly is found only in face-to-face relationships; hence the conviction of ancient Greeks that a life authentically human depended on the city-state and that inhabitants of a giant political order like the Persian Empire could not possibly live as man should. Twentieth-century experience can be interpreted as a confirmation of this assumption. Depersonalization, as in bureaucracy and in statistical habits of mind, is widespread and seems often to be occasioned by the vast numbers of people concentrated in modern cities and nations. Protagonists of community, from Rousseau to Martin Buber, persistently call for decentralization.

So tenacious an attitude is probably not baseless. Nevertheless, community and numbers are not quite so antithetical as defenders of community often suppose. Through inquiring practices and attitudes, a great many people can gain a degree of communal unity. This is exemplified in the international communities of science, art, and literature. Even large-scale politics does not altogether bar community. Our own impersonal times have seen occasions, however brief, when whole peoples have been politically alert and governments exposed to public inquiry.

The cause of community therefore should not be indissolubly linked with that of decentralization. More important and feasible than decentralization is distinguishing and separating communities by type. Thus we prepare ourselves for recognizing and guarding against the inadequacies present in all communal activity. Passing over details, we may note three primary types of community.

1. Political community exists where power is reliably subordinate to common inquiry. This is the case, for example, where laws are passed only after parliamentary debate and where governmental acts are regularly subject to retrospective examination and criticism. Even in the more communal polities, of course, the subordination of government to inquiry is partial and precarious, and some private powers, like corporate business, are normally hidden from public view. Still, the ideal of political community is not unrelated to reality. Occasionally there have been communal institutions, such as the popular courts of ancient Athens and the legislatures in modern democracies, that render governments vulnerable, if not reliably subordinate, to public inquiry. Thus arises politics in the best sense of the term—an activity consisting not merely in the use of power, but in open and rational inquiry into the common good.

The manipulation, violence, and partisanship that enter into politics are unfavorable to community yet render community of particular urgency. Our humanity is at stake in the cultivation of our capacity for communication. Politics poses a crucial test. If we can be communal in our politics, we prove ourselves in the most difficult of circumstances. If we cannot, however, we lay a heavy burden on every other creative activity.

2. Cultural community comes into existence through scientific, historical, artistic, and philosophical inquiry. Cultural community, like political community, comprises the whole of existence. It does this, however, without practical motives.

Herein is the value of cultural community. It demands—whereas political community bars—unreserved truthfulness. In politics the truth is constantly in jeopardy. Not only are some indifferent to the truth, practical considerations may prevent even responsible leaders from telling the truth. A political leader retains honor by not pretending to be invariably candid. But a poet, or anyone else who professes a cultural calling, invites the public to rely on him for even the most inconvenient truths.

Cultural community is in this sense pure community. Its value lies in its unconditionality. Cultural community is inadequate only because human life in actuality is immersed in conditions. The purity of cultural community is unrealistic. It is gained by treating human life as a matter of contemplation alone and not of responsible action as well.

3. Political and cultural communities are public. The most personal, and hence in some ways most communal, relationships, however, are realized in private. Private communities are not defined by content, which may be the same as that of political and cultural communities, but simply by not being public. They are based on a right of exclusion.

Privacy is a right of excluding all persons and all forms of contact and is therefore a right of eschewing community. But the justification for privacy is communal. The right of exclusion is a power of resisting the impurities of political and cultural community. Privacy is degraded when claimed as a right of doing as one pleases. Man's ultimate goal, as recognized in the climactic expressions of both Hellenic and Judaic insight, is a community embracing the entire human race. Yet community would be rarer than it is if we all had to be constantly in the midst of large and miscellaneous assemblages of people. We must be able to choose our relationships and shape our communities. The purpose of the private sphere is to facilitate partial and preparatory realizations of the all-inclusive community that is the human goal.

The three communities—the political, cultural, and private—are interdependent. Each in itself is incomplete. A political community, as we have seen, is chronically infected with untruth. Hence we need the example, discipline, and freedom of a community in which the truth must be spoken regardless of consequences. A cultural community trains participants to frame their utterances with no consideration for practical expedience, and in this way it holds over them a high standard of communal integrity. But it cannot always keep them from the comfortable irresponsibility sometimes evident on the faculties of colleges and universities. Membership in a political community can contribute to the personal balance of someone following a cultural calling.

Finally, both political and cultural communities depend on personalities shaped by the rights and disciplines of privacy. This is obvious in the writers, artists, and thinkers constituting cultural communities. But it is true of political communities as well. A great political leader, such as Abraham Lincoln, may in his personal mystery dwell in solitude. But a personality shaped purely in privacy, shaped by indifference to the worlds illuminated in the political and cultural communities, would be trivial. Private life is only significant as a sphere into which one withdraws and prepares again to go forth.

Merely by marking off as roughly as I have here the basic types of community, we can see that the communal ideal is not anarchistic. Man as a communal being is also a political being. For this to be fully understood, however, we must focus our attention more carefully on political community.

The Structure of Political Community

People not actually engaged in communication may nevertheless be related through a mutual readiness to speak and to listen. Friends are related in this way. Such communal readiness establishes what can be called "interpersonal space"—an area that may be physical, like a legislative chamber, or only metaphorical, like the communal area shared by friends who are far apart.

Political community needs interpersonal space, as do all other communities. Such space has ordinarily been physically defined. The Pnyx in Athens, the hillside on which the Assembly met, and the Forum in Rome were palpable forms of interpersonal space. The quality of a political community may be partially determined by the skill and taste with which the interpersonal space it presupposes is defined; illustrative is the chamber, so conducive both to intimate and to dramatic discourse, where the British House of Commons sits.

The interpersonal space for political communication is not merely physical, however. It is also institutional. One function of a constitution is to define ways in which political communication can occur. The First

Amendment of the American Constitution, providing for freedom of speech and the press and for the right of citizens "peaceably to assemble, and to petition the Government for a redress of grievances," is a charter of interpersonal space. A major source of interpersonal space in the United States today is the presidency; this is due simply to the attention that a president so steadily and effortlessly commands.

The example of the presidency is suggestive. To use interpersonal space to initiate communication is a function of authority. This may at first seem doubtful, for we think of authority as a power of calling forth belief and action rather than a power merely of causing talk. But to command attention and initiate dialogue requires authority. Accordingly we need to distinguish between preemptive authority, which thinks and acts in place of others, and dialogical authority, which inspires and guides discourse. A good teacher possesses dialogical authority, and so does an able political leader. The responsibilities of dialogical authority often are fulfilled mainly by leaders in opposition, by political intellectuals, such as journalists, and by representatives of dissident and underprivileged groups. But one of the greatest powers possessed by the head of a government is that of calling forth and shaping political discourse. This power is exercised not only by speaking but also by acting; political deeds often define the issues of political inquiry. Political leaders should be concerned not just with success but also, when success eludes them, with turning failure into a source of reflection and understanding.

A political community proves itself by compelling mere power to speak and listen, and by reducing preemptive authority to a state of dialogical humility. The way government ministers in Great Britain must day after day appear in the House of Commons with leaders of the opposition, listen to criticism, and in some fashion respond, exhibits dramatically not only the role of authority in political dialogue but also how political institutions may place authorities in inescapably dialogical situations. One of the most serious weaknesses of American political institutions is that a president is never absolutely compelled to speak or listen to his critics.[1] Lord Acton's well-known comment on the corrupting effects of power could be made more specific by saying that

1. See George Reedy, *The Twilight of the Presidency* (New York: World Publishing Co., 1970).

power tends to deprive its possessors of the taste and capacity for inquiring speech. Good political institutions counter this tendency. They provide communal forms and facilities that elites are not at liberty to ignore.

Here we must take into account, however, something similar to inquiry but not exactly the same. Political speech even at its best often promotes only selected truths, only truths favoring the interests of a particular group, party, or class. In these instances it must be classified not as inquiry but as persuasion.

Persuasion may be defined as communication carried on for an end other than truth. It is inquiring in form but activist in substance. Since the ostensible goal of all political communication is discovery of the common good, persuasion always consists in efforts to convince members of the political community that a particular policy is required by the common good. Lacking from persuasion, however, is a fully open and truthful concern for the common good regardless of particular policies and interests. To engage in persuasion is to enter into communal inquiry in behalf of predetermined conclusions. As Martin Buber has said, in authentic communication "no aim, no lust, and no anticipation intervenes between *I* and *Thou*." [2] Persuasion is not authentically communal.

There is good reason for being clear on this. The spirit of communication is rare and fragile, especially in politics. Hence the importance of noting the unique characteristics of communication and shielding it against the urgencies of action. Admittedly, it is often hard to distinguish, even in oneself, between persuasive and communicative concerns; we rarely look for the truth without prior ideas as to what it is or what we would like it to be. Nevertheless, the canons of scientific and scholarly inquiry recognize the difference, and scientists and scholars are expected to take it seriously. When it comes to politics, if the difference is ignored then action and communication are confounded.

If even rational persuasion is not authentically communal, however, we are brought inevitably to a pessimistic conclusion. Political community must be even more fragmentary and ephemeral than it appears to be. Few public figures enter debate only in order to discover the

2. Martin Buber, *I and Thou*, trans. Ronald Gregor Smith (2nd ed.; New York: Charles Scribner's Sons, 1950), 11.

truth. I suggest, nevertheless, that unqualified cynicism would be inappropriate.

Just as scholars and scientists are rarely if ever wholly devoted to the truth, so we may surmise that politicians are rarely if ever wholly indifferent to the truth. Human beings are not so simple as that, and the truth is not so readily abstracted from its manifest utility or its inherent dignity. A participant in political discourse may have predetermined conclusions clearly in view, but evidence and logic have a quiet force and few are exposed to them without being affected. Even in politics, minds sometimes are changed and predetermined conclusions altered or abandoned. Moreover, political leaders often face problems so bewildering that no predetermined conclusions are possible. When that happens, a process of genuine inquiry may begin. Finally, it should be noted that political discourse often is deliberately confined to questions that do not immediately stifle the spirit of inquiry. The role of consensus is a large and unresolved issue among political scientists. But it is certain that wherever there is political community there is also a measure of consensus and that such consensus may concern not only values that everyone accepts but also issues too divisive to be rationally discussed. One function of consensus is to exclude from the public forum questions that would jeopardize the process of communication.

In examining the structure of political community, the basic reason for majority rule becomes apparent. It is not that the majority is necessarily wise. Whether it is a better judge of public issues than various minorities might be is an open question; the answer probably depends usually on the nature of the issue. What majority rule tends to assure is that everyone is addressed. Democracy has less justification as a system of rule than as a system of communication and persuasion. As a system of rule it is subject to most of the failures and inhumanities that attend the use of power by any ruling group. As a system of communication and persuasion, however, it has a unique claim to respect: it is universal.

Universality is not a slight or dispensable advantage. Indeed, it is not properly speaking an advantage at all, but rather a moral imperative implicit in the very concept of political community. It is, however, an imperative that cannot be fully met. The tension that thus arises, the tension between the universality of the communal ideal and the limits imposed by political actualities, is our primary experience of the contradictory character of political community. Only if we understand this tension can we understand the paradoxical obligation of communal man: not to seek the pure community of an anarchistic paradise but to accept the compromised community available in the polity.

Liberation and Its Limits

The ideal of political community logically generates an effort to set everyone free for communication. Where this does not occur, the determination rationally to seek the truth has been curbed—perhaps in order to protect the power of a dominant group, perhaps from contempt for average people. Whatever the reason, political communication is under constraint. Inquiry is implicitly universal. If there are people to whom I am unwilling to speak or to listen, then I am in some measure and way either indifferent to the truth or else absolutely sure that I already possess it. I cannot care for the truth and be cognizant of my own fallibility without listening to all voices.

To will a universal community, however, requires more than attentiveness and availability. It requires taking action to remove obstacles to communication, and these obstacles are not only legal but also economic, social, and educational. In a word, the pursuit of truth implies an egalitarian and radical bias. Rank and exclusion, as common as they are in intellectual life, require justification as exceptions. And communication, although differing essentially from action, gives rise in most circumstances to imperatives of action; it demands not only the spirit, but care for the social and material conditions, of communication. The ideal of community thus is an ideal of liberation.

Here, however, we encounter the contradiction at the core of political community. Efforts at liberation can never fully succeed and probably can never come near to succeeding. This is owing both to limits inherent in action and to defects in the human beings who act. These conditions must be closely examined if we are to understand the relationship between the individual and the political community.

We may conveniently begin with the limits inherent in action (as distinguished from the defects of those who act). These must be assessed with particular care, for modern man places extreme reliance on his powers of action, and this is perilous. The ideal of community strongly moves us. It symbolizes the end of loneliness and desolation.

Hence misunderstandings and false promises concerning the prospects of community are seductive. They can draw us into disastrous plans and efforts.

If community is inquiry, it cannot be a political creation. It may be encouraged by action but cannot be deliberately produced. Enforcing racial integration in the schools, for example, or supporting the best television programs with public funds are reasonably calculated to contribute to communication. But there can be no assurance that they really will. Action must terminate in an external arrangement, and between the external arrangement and the communication that it is designed to produce there is a gap that can be filled only by spontaneity. This gap requires what might be called "an interval of inaction."

Community is something we must wait for, once favorable conditions have been created. The interval of inaction is an interval of attentiveness and is imposed by the inseparability of truth and inquiry as expressed in the ideal of community. It is often said that after a period of reform there must be a period of quiescence during which the changes made can be "digested." The main moral content of this assertion lies perhaps in its affirmation of the possible value of inaction. That value of course is not assured; and inaction on the part of a government always derives some support from questionable motives. But one sign of wisdom in the design of the American Constitution is the way it favors a rhythm of historical movement, a rhythm in which periods of change, while often perhaps not as consequential as they should be, are not indefinitely prolonged.

But an interval of inaction need not be entered into simultaneously by all agents of a society and government. Indeed, an interval of inaction need not even be a perceptible period of quiescence. It may consist rather in a spirit of mutuality, in a realization among leaders that their effectiveness depends on responses they can hope for but cannot assure. Tyrants infuriated by the slightest opposition exemplify the difficulty of inaction. All of us yearn for command of our lives and are touched by rage when command is denied us. The interval of inaction means that rage is suppressed, and the craving for command is replaced by hope.

Inaction ought even to be a kind of ideal—a goal toward which action is directed. Not that inaction itself is what anyone desires. But if human nature is communal, and community is inquiry, then inaction is our only access to what we do desire. We cannot move straight to our goals. We act for the sake of fruitful inaction. This does not mean that we should act very little; modern politics inevitably entails a great deal of action. But wise action is indirect. It aims at creating a state of affairs in which attentiveness and availability alone—communality without action—constitute a reasonable and hopeful stance.

If inaction is an ideal, then ideals other than inaction must have a different place in our lives than is ordinarily given them. Our immediate aim should not be to realize particular ideals but rather to establish a communal freedom in which ideals can be formed and rationally considered. The major flaw in every utopia is that ideals are given priority over inquiry. Communication consequently is severely limited or altogether excluded—often in the name of community. A notorious instance is the utopia delineated by so great an inquirer as Plato, a utopia leaving little room for the communality represented by Socrates.

If community is prior to ideals, it is prior to justice. Contrary to assumptions common among people dedicated to liberation, we should not act to establish justice but rather to establish conditions under which we can collectively inquire into justice—into its nature and into the imperatives it implies in the existing situation. Radicals are suspicious (on good grounds) of those who want to think about justice rather than immediately to establish it. First justice, then community, is the radical rule. But communication thus is reduced to a mere diversion. If communication is not for discovering the nature and requirements of justice, what importance does it have?

Communication is prior even to theorems concerning the conditions of communication. It is not possible to specify a particular form of society either as absolutely incompatible with communication or as universally necessary if communication is to occur. If it were, man would not be that mysterious creature who can only be communicatively encountered and not definitively known. The dangers in Marx's thought are closely connected with this point. It is true that Marx was experimental and undogmatic in looking ahead, beyond the overthrow of capitalism. He did not burden the future with prior designs. He did, however, burden the present with a dogma concerning the conditions of communication. Serious and sustained communication could not occur in a capitalist system; the common good could not be communally discovered or change peacefully accomplished. In this way man was treated as an object of absolute knowledge and, fatefully, of revolutionary action.

Our powers of action are not limited only by the character of action itself, however. They are limited also by the character of man. With few if any exceptions (although in varying degrees), human beings are preoccupied with their own welfare and standing. Even if all outer obstacles to community were removed, there would remain the great inner obstacles of selfishness and pride. These in a multitude of ways obscure the truth and obstruct communication. They enhance the difficulty of seeing reality as others see it; they cause one to recoil before the humbling experience of admitting error; they lend power greater charm than truth.

Selfishness and pride greatly increase the risks of inaction. Facing an interval of inaction we must acknowledge not merely the need for time but the possibility of failure.

Man's deep and persistent self-concern does not merely jeopardize the results of wise actions, however; it means also that many actions will not be wise. Decisions will be made on the basis of one-sided views of reality; they will be derived from dogmas that those in power are unwilling either to surrender or to expose to common inquiry; and they will be calculated with greater concern for domination than for inquiry.

It is often held, or at least assumed, that man's moral imperfections will sometime disappear. It is often argued that they are produced by social circumstances and will be rectified with the progress of social reform. Of course the very possibility of such progress, to be accomplished by a being whose moral imperfection is postulated in the hypothesis itself, is open to doubt. But let us admit that *social* progress, the perfecting of society, is possible; *moral* progress, the perfecting of man, is a different matter. This can be shown by three observations.

1. Preoccupation with one's own welfare and standing is primarily a response to insecurity—an insecurity that is most obviously, but not exclusively, physical and that, although affected by society, is in its basic forms ontological. Social progress can lessen the risks of daily life but cannot eliminate our finitude or mortality. Hence in all imaginable social circumstances we shall be powerfully tempted by selfishness and pride.

2. The very project of moral improvement is more dubious than often supposed. You cannot refashion yourself morally, for you cannot gain a fully transcendent or morally pure vantage point from which this task might be undertaken. Our finitude and our very imperfections undercut efforts toward self-improvement.

3. Even if individuals do make moral progress, they have no way of transmitting their gains to their descendants. Moral excellence cannot, like inherited biological characteristics or technical knowledge, be passed on to posterity. Manners can be improved, but later generations can hardly be born onto a morally more elevated plane than the generations preceding them.

In sum, moral imperfection is not like a troublesome disease that can be scientifically studied and deliberately eradicated. It may not belong to the human essence, but it is fixed in the human situation and character in such a way that its passing is hard to imagine.

Even if our moral faults could be finally overcome, however, our finitude would remain. Finitude means confinement to particular spatial and temporal locations. Our knowledge is necessarily limited in extent and shaped by our circumstances and traditions. The unification of consciousness, as noted in Chapter II, is always a venture, never a definitive result. In consequence, even if our motives were pure, our actions would invariably have unforeseen and undesired results. Sometimes they would be destructive. Finitude means that human action is always in a measure blind.

All of this brings us to the conclusion that man as a political being is under an imperative of liberation to which he cannot fully respond. Political life embodies a moral impasse. Nowhere is the tragic character of community more apparent than in the political sphere. Nowhere, consequently, are there stronger temptations to indulge in illusions. One of our major political responsibilities is simply to resist these illusions and remember our condition.

Imperatives of Imperfection

To remember our condition is to keep our political outlook firmly dualistic. Some of the requisite dualities have come up in the course of our reflections. There is, for example, the duality of *action and inquiry*. Even a perfect process of inquiry could not demonstrate the validity of ultimate values; much less could any actual process of inquiry do this. Nor can inquiry fully illuminate the circumstances in which values are sought. Hence never, through political dialogue, do we come to know incontestably what we should do, and action is always undertaken in a state of rational uncertainty. Another duality is that of *domination and communication*. If communication involves "no aim, no lust, and no anticipation," it must be sharply distinguished from every form of domination—even, as earlier seen, domination exercised through persuasion. Finally, note may be taken of a duality implied in the opening section of this chapter, namely, *politics and culture*. The proposition that the political and cultural communities should be separate arises from a recognition that politics is a matter of action and domination, whereas culture is governed by standards of inquiry and communication.

Our natural desire to harmonize and simplify tempts us to fuse these polar spheres, thus obscuring the inevitability and evil of power and denying the enduring role and dignity of the critical mind. Ideologies are always in the final analysis monistic and hence delusory. Dualities like those mentioned above contradict ideological illusions of harmony and simplicity. They remind us of the kind of world we inhabit. The "imperatives of imperfection" are simply those involved in guarding the dualistic structure of the political mind.

The imperatives concerning our attitudes toward action, domination, and politics might be summarized simply by saying that power must not be idealized. This may sound easy, but the history of political thought and action shows that it is not. The basic facts of power—its indispensability and its inhumanity—reflect badly on our character and prospects. It is tempting to brighten the picture we have of ourselves and the future by envisioning the full humanization or the disappearance of power. Rousseau did the former (in his concept of the general will), Marx the latter.

Recalling some elementary distinctions may help to clarify our thinking. Mere power is the brute fact of interpersonal control, whereas authority is power that is willingly accepted. Authority is often spoken of as though it were essentially legitimate. For power simply to be willingly accepted, however, does not make it legitimate. Authority may, after all, rest on ignorance and illusions. Authority can be fully legitimate only if it rests on unconstrained rationality—on inquiry not compromised by such conditions as media of information that are corrupt and biased and schools that neglect the techniques and disciplines of common reasoning. On these grounds, we may distinguish power, illegitimate authority, and legitimate authority. Such distinctions are not unacceptable to common sense. They contain at least one implication, however, that is seldom noted by common sense.

If legitimate and illegitimate authority be distinguished as I have suggested, it follows that practically all authority is more or less illegitimate. Not that mere power everywhere prevails. In order to last and be effective, power must be accepted by those over whom it is exercised; it must take the form of authority. But authority everywhere depends on a measure of prejudice, sloth, and other civil deficiencies. Indeed the very conditions that necessitate authority—the lack of full rationality and mutual understanding, that is, imperfections of community—deprive existing authorities of complete legitimacy.

This does not imply of course that we must live in a state of continuous rebellion. It does not require that we never obey but only that we obey with a realization that all preemptive authority is morally dubious. We should support conditions that cultivate civic consciousness and temper authority; we should insist on constitutionalism—on the subordination of authority to reliable limits.

Above all, we should be steadily and radically critical in our relations with government and law. If full legitimacy depends on unconstrained rationality, authority is legitimate only in the degree to which it is open to rational challenge. Although a government cannot permit disobedience or revolutionary action, a government that does not allow these to be advocated in speech interferes with rational inquiry into its own foundations and thus lessens its legitimacy. It must be granted that lines of demarcation in this area are difficult to draw; recommending revolution and actually working for revolution, for example, are not always easily distinguished. It must be granted too, in view of human selfishness and pride, that governments cannot always afford to be casual about threats to their prestige and stability. These qualifications only underscore the proposition that authority rarely if ever is fully legitimate, for it is difficult to see how full legitimacy can be gained except by exposure to unlimited critical inquiry.

In a manner of speaking, the first imperative of imperfection is political mistrust. The second imperative of imperfection is something logically incumbent on those who are subject to illegitimate authority—that is to keep alive the activity of inquiry or communication. Doing this depends on intellectual mistrust—on viewing skeptically every supposedly comprehensive and apodictic theory of society.

Liberation therefore is experimental. No one today would deny that Marxism and psychoanalysis can help us to understand the ways in which people are trammeled and confined by society and the ways in which they can be freed. But for many these persuasions have been converted into pseudo-scientific illusions. They have been construed as infallible doctrines of liberation.

Liberation is not only experimental, it is also historically inconclusive. It is not an activity by means of which a liberated society at last will come into existence. Through liberation, men may approach community; but they never reach it, and what they do in addition is to meet the demanding task of living humanely in history. Like Lessing's truth, the glory lies not in the results alone but in the search as well.

The idea of capitalism has played a particularly important role among the false finalities that have plagued the world in recent times. First came the affirmation of capitalism. It was put forward as an organizational principle of unqualified validity. Not many are still persuaded by that affirmation. Some, however, have simply reversed it. If not the unique source of most of the values that society is organized to secure, capitalism produces most of the evils from which society suffers. No longer historically ultimate, it is penultimate: its destruction will open the way to justice and community. In a time when objects that can be unqualifiedly accepted are hard to find, capitalism serves for many as the next-best thing, an object that can be unqualifiedly rejected.

Negative finalities are no less antithetical to inquiry, however, than are positive finalities. This is illustrated by capitalism, the value of which cannot be summarized in a simple affirmation or negation. Thus the classical economists were right to a degree. Free markets can be both efficient and just, and socialists have still not demonstrated the practicality of their ideal alternatives. Capitalism has even contributed to community by creating widespread prosperity and supporting constitutional government. But Marxists also are right to a degree. Capitalism is anticommunal in principle by relying on markets rather than communal inquiry; it is anticommunal in practice by forcing everyone to give priority to power rather than to truth. Thus capitalism is filled with ambiguities requiring inquiry.

The issue of capitalism is typical. To maintain our communality we must on most big issues say both yes and no. Many hunger for the certitude that comes from unhesitating and irrevocable decisions. To satisfy them, however, would be to do away with doubts inseparable from earthly community. It would be to liquidate communal politics.

Is it now apparent why that must not be allowed to happen—why our humanity is involved, not in a communal purity that sets one apart from the world, but rather in bearing the tensions of political community?

The Claims of Political Community

Politics meets a standard of communality noted in the preceding chapter: it engages the interest of man as he is in essence. This is not because of the opportunities it offers for garnering honor or because of powers it provides for changing the world. These are the premises of ancient and modern political man. It is rather because politics encompasses all human life (being in this way "the queen of the arts and sciences," as Aristotle asserted) and that it does this from the standpoint of our responsibility for shaping and guarding that life. In politics we deliberate upon human existence as an object of action. An occasion thus is provided for a communality unique in its range and gravity.

But these qualities are, so to speak, perfections of political community. The imperfections of political community also, paradoxically, give rise to claims on participatory activity. In its comprehensiveness, a political community is responsible for harmony among its constituent groups. With its monopoly of force, it must resolve coercively all issues that cannot be resolved spontaneously. Hence a political community becomes a repository of communal deficiencies and an agency of force. How can such a situation be a source of moral claims?

For one thing, only as participants in a polity do we fully face the necessity of action. Although community and action are antithetical, they also are inseparable; as we have seen, communication necessitates action because it depends on conditions we can deliberately affect. Communication that ignores the necessity of action is abstracted from the world and history and consequently is false. We prove our strength and truthfulness as communal beings only by confronting our practical responsibilities, and this we do only as members of a political community.

Moreover, political community is where we come to terms not only with action but also with its invariable accompaniment, power. It is true of power, as of action, that only by acknowledging its necessity, experiencing its reality, and struggling to subordinate it to communication can we prove our strength and truthfulness as communal beings. Many of the most fervent advocates of community have closed their eyes to power. In some instances they have denied the very need for government, calling for the abolition of the state or foreseeing its "withering away"; in other instances they have obscured the ugliness and inevitability of power by raising up ideals of perfect democracy. This is understandable. It reflects sensitivity to the offense of power and the nature of community. But it reflects also an unwillingness to face historical conditions. Community is affirmed, but not as a reality in the world. Hence it is not an association of concrete human beings—not an authentic community—that is affirmed. That is done only by accepting and taking part in a community that is truly political, that is, structured—and inevitably compromised—by the presence of power.

Only in the polity do we fully experience community as a tragic ideal. It can be genuine community we thus experience—the most comprehensive of communities and one not necessarily diluted into unreality by the multitudes it must embrace—but it is community weakened and disfigured, as well as upheld, by action and power.

To live lucidly within a political community depends on sustaining the tension between liberation and its limits. We possess integrity as communal beings only if we act wherever possible to create the conditions on which community depends. But we retain our availability for community and our openness to others in their full historical concreteness only by realizing that all action, even action in behalf of community, has anticommunal consequences. We cannot live either as uncompromising liberators or as unyielding defenders of the existing order. Our responsibilities as communal beings are more complicated and more onerous.

These reflections bring us to a position diametrically opposed to

Aristotle. We cannot expect harmonious fulfillment of our potentialities through participation in political community. This is because we cannot expect, where there is politics, to find community except with the tragic imperfections inherent in earthly and historical existence. What we gain through political community is only a clear consciousness of our character and situation—communal but inescapably estranged. This, however, is not a slight claim in behalf of political community. It enables us to agree with Aristotle in one respect. Even though man does not fulfill his potentialities in political community—indeed, *because* of this fact and the insights it provides—he remains a political being. Through politics he realizes something more important than his potentialities—his humanity.

IV / EQUALITY AND THE WILL TO UNITY

Human beings are moved by a compelling desire for unity—a desire to eliminate loose ends and clarify uncertain connections, to simplify and synthesize. The manifestations of this desire in the universe of society and politics are multifarious. It underlies both authoritarianism and democracy; it can be secular or religious and was evident both in the Roman Empire and the Christian Church; it is represented in political ideals as divergent as Plato's doctrine of philosophical kingship and Marx's prophecy of proletarian victory; it is present in the modern totalitarian state but also in the longing for peace and world understanding.

The will to unity is morally ambiguous. It can be on the side of community, as it is when its ends are truth and common inquiry or the social grounds on which common inquiry is likely to occur. On the other hand, it can signify only that we wish for a world under our command or a world so simple and orderly that it does not trouble us to think or engage in communication. In this form, exemplified by movements, sometimes revolutionary and sometimes conservative, toward order undisturbed by diversity or dissent, the will to unity is destructive of community.

Unfortunately, it is difficult to distinguish between the healthy and the destructive forms of the will to unity. The communal impulse is readily diverted. Social unity temporarily alleviates the pain of estrangement and thus may be eagerly accepted in place of community. In the early years of the Third Reich, few Nazis can have been aware that what they were involved in was not a community; loneliness was assuaged and for the moment that sufficed. Further, the very fact that social unity can be willed encourages man to identify it with community. It is exasperating to have to wait, without assurance, for something one desperately desires.

The confusion might be more easily avoided if pure dedication to community were possible. But it is not; social unity is a matter of practical urgency. Merely to meet our needs as physical beings we must create social forms facilitating cooperation. A safe singleness of mind is impossible.

Owing to this situation, the proper care of plurality is essential to the art of politics. To avoid the fatal confusion of social unity and community, it is imperative to cultivate and guard plurality. Unity, of course, is important too. Human beings cannot address one another unless they share common circumstances, symbols, and goals. But neither can they address one another without differences and distances of various kinds. Hence the art of politics consists in knowing how to care for unity, yet in knowing also how and when to resist the will to unity, guarding and encouraging plurality. Comparing two revolutionary leaders, Washington practised the true art of politics, simultaneously realizing and curbing the will to unity in the Constitution, whereas Lenin did not and perhaps, in his circumstances, could not.

One issue of particular difficulty and importance faces us today in trying to deal wisely with the will to unity; it is that of equality *versus* inequality. The ideal of equality has probably done more than anything else in the modern world to activate and empower the will to unity. Not that equality is essentially opposed to community. Rank fades away among those who seriously address and pay attention to one another. Man's desire for community thus is implicitly egalitarian. Nonetheless, equality is readily, often inevitably, understood as social unity. When this happens it instills a deep reluctance to curb the drive toward unity and await community.

The ideal of equality, like the will to unity, is dangerously ambiguous. It has immense moral authority, for without equality there can be no community. At the same time, it often inspires an unrestrained will to unity, thus in fact opposing community. It is a hard ideal to handle because it can be neither repudiated nor unreservedly accepted. It presents a severe test of our good judgment and our concern for community.

This test is often imposed on us by radicalism, which typically takes the form of an unqualified commitment to equality. Radicalism addresses us with a formidable voice. It speaks not only with the authority inherent in the ideal of equality but also with the power deriving from man's yearning for community. It disturbs the contentment of those who would gladly ignore the standard of equality and acquiesce in the flagrant violations of that standard occurring in modern industrial societies. The trouble with radicalism, in its typical forms, lies in the absence of reservations. Radicals are inclined to view with contempt those who do not insist on equality, established if necessary with force. In other words, they are contemptuous of the art of politics.

It is my aim in the following pages to reflect on the problem of pursuing equality without being drawn into ruinous efforts at social unification. At the outset we must consider the general nature of society. We must try to identify those characteristics that place it in opposition to community and also to see where equality and inequality belong among those characteristics.

The Roots of Society

Aristotle asserts that men join together for the sake of mere life; concern for the *good* life comes later. This is a simple and unassuming statement, but it contains an important insight. Society is rooted in physical necessity—although, as we shall see, not in physical necessity alone. Societies must exist for the human race to survive, and each of us must be a member of society in order to live.

Dangers to physical existence have two primary sources—man and nature. Hence there are two basic necessities—protection against men and utilization of nature. Both necessities are equally compelling; man cannot live without both defending and exploiting a portion of the earth. To do these things, he must join with others. Society is necessarily a military and economic order.

"Order," however, is a word with connotations of stability, and these should not be allowed to obscure the fact that society is organized for the sake of action. People enter into society to accomplish certain goals, to change and control the realities around them. When we reflect on military and economic order, therefore, we are concerned with arrangements for facilitating collective action. From this standpoint, it is possible to identify four primary characteristics of society.

First, society is an organization or system and cannot be merely a spontaneous assemblage. Only an organization can effectively act. Of course the power of organized society over individuals can be restricted. Constitutionalism is supposed to do this, and a constitutional polity is likely to contain individuals and groups that are more or less dissociated from common goals and patterns of action. Nevertheless, society as a coherent system of action has behind it the force of necessity. Hence those guiding it are both naturally disposed and morally obliged continually to ask how much dissociation of this kind can be afforded.

Society, then, has an inherent tendency to become monistic and totalitarian. This is reflected in the position of artists and writers. Artistic and literary creativity tend to unsettle and individualize people, to make them less thoughtless and hence less reliable parts in the social machine. The ruling powers therefore are disposed to subordinate such creativity to the forms of respectable culture. When military and economic pressures are light, and there is peace and plenty, society can relax its hold. But in times of military tension or economic urgency artists and writers are apt to be mobilized along with all others.

Second, organized for action, society is ceaselessly involved in the objective and expediential assessment of reality that we may call "appraisal." There is only limited room for the leisured speaking and listening in which nothing more is sought than common understanding. Society must in this way set itself against community. It must appraise foreign peoples in order to ascertain their military intentions and capabilities; it must appraise its own members to determine the contributions they can make to military and economic undertakings; it must appraise the portion of the earth that it occupies. As some avoid being mobilized, of course, some stand outside the sphere of appraisal. So far as artists and writers seek to express personal visions rather than gain positions in society, they stand in the sphere of community. But they are not often so pure in their motives, nor are they often left free to be. The subordination of artistic creativity to appraisal is illustrated in nineteenth-century France, where impressionist painters faced an entrenched style, dominating all major exhibitions, and providing an avenue by which those uncreative or opportunistic enough to follow it could gain wealth and prestige.

Third, if society is an organization and a sphere of appraisal, it inevitably raises a minority to the status of sovereign organizers and appraisers. It is difficult to imagine how stable and effective social order could exist without hierarchies of organizers and appraisers. Not only must there be government and arms, both entailing inequalities of power, there must probably be inequalities of wealth as well. Today, even if the giant corporations were broken up, there would still be large concentrations of property, such as factories. These must be controlled by someone—if not by private owners, then by civil servants or leading workers. Inherent in their positions would be power and prestige at the very least, and it would be a decided novelty in the history of the human race were there not privileges and luxuries too.

Finally, society is necessarily moved by a logic of largeness. Other things being equal, the more numerous a society the stronger, both militarily and economically, it will be. Earlier reflections suggested that numbers and community are not wholly incompatible; a very large society might be united by common attentiveness. But community on a large scale must be severely diluted in comparison with a relationship in which another person (using a phrase with which Martin Buber characterizes the "I—Thou" relationship) "fills the sky." Large numbers lend themselves to various forms of appraisal, such as statistical calculation, as small numbers do not. Hence it must be said that size is unfavorable to community. The fall of the Greek city-states before the empires of Macedonia and of Rome was a tragedy of numbers. With their tiny populations they could be relatively communal, but they were also weak.

To organize and appraise, to place some people over others, to bring together large numbers of people: all of these are more or less opposed to community, even though community could not exist without them. This can be seen in some of the ways society acts on consciousness.

Society tends to cultivate and maintain a state of mind in which estrangement is implicit. It does this primarily by opposing unrestricted inquiry, the common search for truth that is at the heart of community. It may promote scientific inquiry, but it is likely to resist the kind of inquiry carried on in philosophy and art. There seem to be two basic reasons for this and correspondingly two basic types of distorted consciousness that society encourages.

In the first place, society artificially reinforces the kind of consciousness that is determined primarily by everyday experience and is usually referred to as "common sense." Since society is organized for the sake of action, it depends on a widespread willingness to accept as reality whatever is disclosed in ordinary practical experience. Vision is threatening. This helps to explain the hostility with which both communist and capitalist societies have reacted to absract art—why even so austere a painter as Cézanne was sometimes treated like a dangerous revolutionary. He tended to subvert the dominion of common sense and to show that everyday experience does not comprise the totality of being.

At the same time, societies are apt to support the kind of consciousness—antithetical both to common sense and to vision—that can be embodied in an ideology. Human beings cannot live wholly on common sense; they need ideas pertaining to man's basic nature and ultimate destiny. And they would prefer not to live on inquiry; they are attracted to ideas that are simple and encouraging, ideas that do not burden them with reservations and doubts. An ideology deals with both historical causes and ultimate values and is an ostensibly complete and unquestionable guide to common action. Hence its utility for society. It arouses dedication to public purposes and promotes cohesion. It inclines people to lend themselves willingly to organization and appraisal. While encouraging unity, of course, an ideology tends to stifle the common quest for truth that is community. It calls for a willful consolidation of consciousness.

The two forms of distorted consciousness may of course come into conflict. This happened when Nazi Germany expelled some nuclear scientists because they were Jewish. Society is impelled by its own inherent logic, however, to promote both types of consciousness. To act effectively, it needs both practicality and unity. It does not need, and often has trouble accommodating, community.

In discussing ideology we have come to something that exists because man is a being whose needs are not merely physical. Of course no sharp line can be drawn between man's activities as a physical and a spiritual being; in trying to meet his physical needs he behaves as the spiritual being that he is, and in behaving as a spiritual being he retains his physical needs. We can nevertheless distinguish between the physical and spiritual roots of society, as Aristotle did when he said that although society "*grows* for the sake of mere life, it *exists* for the sake of a good life."[1]

Society provides forms through which human beings enter into relations with those realities that, using Tillich's expression, are matters of ultimate concern. Through culture they dedicate themselves to the vision gained and expressed in literature, art, and philosophy; through religion they reach toward and act upon faith. As culture and religion, society is a spiritual order. Following Aristotle, we may say that although society is occasioned by physical need its purpose is spiritual.

Society does more for community, then, than merely keeping us alive. It provides forms for communication. What must be emphasized in the present context, however, is that this does not alter essentially the structure of society that arises from physical necessity. For one thing, the patterns of domination and the habits of mind that arise from physical necessity are not left altogether behind in the cultural and religious realms. As exemplified in the power of the bourgeoisie in art museums and churches, the appraisers and organizers who supervise our response to physical necessity have much to say about our spiritual activities.

However, even if the cultural and religious realms were altogether unaffected by economic and military power, they would still be structured hierarchically for appraisal and organization. Such is the nature of society. Whatever the purposes served, action of some kind is envisaged; whether the field of action is physical or spiritual, human beings must be appraised and organized. The results are apparent in almost any cultural or ecclesiastical association. Even the forms of distorted consciousness that society supports in order to meet physical needs are apt to be encouraged also within spiritual associations; thus, corresponding with common sense in society at large, is realism in art and literature, and corresponding with ideology is religious dogma.

In sum, as Marx and others have shown, society as a spiritual order is less elevated than some have supposed. It is debased both by the influence of society as an order for meeting physical needs and by the fact that it is in itself a form of social order, hence governed by the imperatives of organization, appraisal, hierarchy and numbers.

1. *The Politics of Aristotle*, trans. Ernest Barker (Oxford: Clarendon Press, 1946), 5.

Up to this point, the concept of necessity has dominated our reflections. We are not merely victims of necessity, however; we are also its willing allies. To organize and appraise, to rule over others, is for most of us an agreeable task. Hence we conspire with necessity. We not only do what necessity requires, but more. We organize and appraise, we gather together larger and larger numbers, for the exhilaration of ascendancy. To use a word that is old-fashioned but incomparably precise, society is rooted not just in necessity but also in sin.

The primary form of sin is pride—the persistent tendency of each one to exalt himself over all others. If pride stimulates organization and appraisal, the converse also is true. Society, with its hierarchies of organization and appraisal, powerfully encourages pride. The supreme organizers and appraisers, given not only power but also wealth and rank and set over depersonalized multitudes, are likely to think of themselves as more intelligent and noble than ordinary people. It is difficult in the most favorable circumstances to be unreservedly attentive and available. When office and possessions exalt one above others, imposing duties of appraisal and control, it is almost impossible; the needed humility cannot survive. Thus it is that "power tends to corrupt," and that "it is easier for a camel to go through the eye of a needle, than for a rich man to enter into the kingdom of God." [2]

Society is also connected with a moral disorder at the opposite pole from pride—self-abandonment. While people love to be organizers and appraisers, they also love, perhaps from weariness or fear, to be organized and appraised. It is a relief from the burden of selfhood to become immersed in tasks that others have chosen and in routines that others have framed. Those who embrace whatever role and purpose society offers, tacitly deify the social order. Society is a plausible god, vast enough to seem infinite and enduring enough to seem eternal. The totalitarian state is the most obvious and extreme example of the deification of society, and totalitarianism is possible only when multitudes of people are prepared for self-abandonment. But every society is a god to some of those within it.

Thus man makes either too much of himself or too little, slighting either his finitude or his freedom and responsibility. Considering the passion and determination with which in these ways he denies his hu-

2. Matthew 19:24

manity, we are justified in viewing skeptically the Marxist expectation that technological progress will finally free man from the imperatives of physical necessity and thus from patterns of behavior antithetical to community. Although man's readiness to enlist in hierarchies of appraisal and organization accords conveniently with the imperatives of physical necessity, it does not appear to be altogether the product of those imperatives.

But in any case, how can pride and the inclination to self-abandonment ever fail to find footing in the hard ground of physical necessity? The Marxist assumption that technological progress will eventually free us from technological constraints is no less dubious than the assumption that in doing this it would free us from sin as well. Technology in many ways renders the constraints of society more numerous and compelling. A highly organized social order is an absolute prerequisite to large-scale industry, and organization becomes more rational and intensive under the spur of industrial development. Appraisal is apt to become more refined, dispassionate, and comprehensive under the influence of technological requirements and habits of mind. As technology advances, inequality is upheld not only, as always, by necessity and ambition but also by the dependence of technological order on a highly developed system of management and expertise. And technology greatly facilitates the governance of vast numbers.

Marxists assume that material plenty will contribute to our liberation from technological constraints, but it is difficult to see why this should happen. Only by our accepting such constraints is material plenty gained. Even if economic imperatives could be met with a relatively slight expenditure of time and energy, those imperatives would be inviolable and constant. And everywhere they would invite pride and self-abandonment.

Technology provides ways in which human beings can assert themselves and lose themselves more fully than ever before. There were tyrannies in ancient times but nothing like the kind of domination made possible by modern industrial organization and modern communications media. Wars have been made more lethal and consuming. Whole populations are looked upon as matériel.

The dangers inherent in the will to unity can now be more clearly seen. That will is supported by physical necessity and spiritual striving, and by ambition and despair. It issues in hierarchies of organization and appraisal, and in efforts to amass human beings underneath those hierarchies. Technology contains at least as many potentialities for worsening as for bettering this situation. These conclusions do not dictate despair, but they do point to the importance of curbing the will to unity. They point to the importance of plurality.

The Principle of Plurality

No social entity—no group, institution, or authority—should be uncriticized or allowed to provide the total environment for human beings. No ideology or policy should receive unqualified allegiance. Each person should belong to different groups, heed various authorities, and consider diverse social and political prescriptions. This, briefly, is the principle of plurality.

It seems to me the mark of a deep misunderstanding that the ideal of community has been so often set in opposition to the principle of plurality. This happened very clearly in Rousseau, with his condemnation of separate powers, parties, and groups within the state. The source of this misunderstanding, I suggest, is that of making far too mundane and ordinary a thing out of community. The most perfect unity human beings can know, that found in searching together for the truth, is either forgotten or condemned. It is supposed that one who chooses the freedom and the rare but incomparable comradeship of that search has turned away from community. The result on the one hand is that cohesive social entities, such as small towns or ethnic neighborhoods—at best satisfying but unintellectual, at worst oppressive and antiintellectual—are dignified as communities. On the other hand the activity of comprehensive and probing communication is treated with negligence or disapproval—and this, strangely enough, by proponents of "community."

One of the oldest and best-known expressions of the principle of plurality is the doctrine of the separation of church and state. It is remarkable that this doctrine received its earliest and perhaps clearest formulation from a pope—from Gelasius, who in the fifth century set forth the so-called "doctrine of the two swords." By sanctioning two more or less separate authorities, the spiritual and the temporal,

Gelasius tacitly acknowledged that even the Catholic Church should not wield the only "sword" over man or provide the total environment of its members.

But if the spiritual sword should not govern all of life, spiritual as well as temporal, why should it govern all *spiritual* life? Why should there be just one spiritual sword? Tacitly conceding limitations on the part of the Church, the doctrine of the two swords implied the legitimacy of a plurality of churches. This implication has been drawn only slowly and reluctantly within the churches and even today is accepted less than wholeheartedly. It did not enter into the thinking of the Reformers, and Protestants no less than Catholics typically speak longingly of the unification of the churches. But if churches, like other social entities, involve hierarchies for organization and appraisal, it seems fitting that there should be diversity among them. It also seems fitting that various cultural associations, such as universities, should exist beyond the boundaries of the churches.

As for the temporal realm, it has long been accepted that here a plurality of swords should govern. As far back as the Middle Ages, political plurality was commonplace both in theory and in practice. In the modern world it has been institutionalized in such forms as independent courts and competing parties.

The principle of plurality can be applied not only to institutions but also to policies and programs. History is littered with the wreckage of policies that collapsed when societies put their full weight on them. To go back only a hundred years, it used to be argued by intelligent men that justice, as well as the utmost efficiency, could be realized through strict adherence to a policy of *laissez-faire*. When this was tried, however, human relationships were ravaged by acquisitiveness and inequality. Socialism arose with the precise aim of subordinating economic relationships to community. But socialist critics of *laissez-faire* often themselves fell under the spell of a single policy, such as the nationalization of industry. That policy, we can now see, assures only that appraisal and organization will be carried on by bureaucrats rather than by businessmen. A society ought to contain two or more political parties not so much in order that the best policy will be devised but to keep alive the consciousness that no policy is wholly satisfactory.

The principle of plurality can be stated negatively. Just as there is no historical entity or policy that is a reliable source of pure community, neither is there any historical entity or policy that is the sole or primary source of estrangement. The idea that there is represents one of the most treacherous devices of pride. This is illustrated by Marxism. Marx was contemptuous of state idolatry and expressed this both in his critique of bourgeois governments as class dictatorships and in his prediction that under communism the state would disappear. He was also properly mistrustful of human designs and policies, as can be seen in his denunciation of utopian socialism. In short, Marx accepted some of the basic attitudes I have expressed in terms of the principle of plurality. But Marx thought that he had identified the one major source of estrangement: the class conflict that supposedly arose from the institution of private property and had come to a climax in the capitalist system. Thus he involved himself in a kind of negative idolatry. The result, for all of Marx's stress on economics, was to obscure the primal, enduring character of the necessities inherent in physical existence. The result also was to deny implicitly the persistence of pride and of the inclination to self-abandonment. It was implied that with the collapse of capitalism and of economic classes, and with the abolition of private property, full community would come into existence. It was also implied that a few—those lifted to leadership by the rising tide of the proletariat—could be relied upon as the destroyers of capitalism and the founders of community. Marx did not explicitly draw such inferences, but many of his followers did and in this way became involved in the idolatry of state and policy that Marx had scorned.

The typical upshot of communal political theory is a myth of perfect and palpable unity—the limitless rule of a scientific and philosophic elite (Plato), of a morally pure and politically undivided populace (Rousseau), of a historically predestined party (Lenin). The necessities and the human imperfections that enter into the formation of societies are forgotten, and community and social unity are confounded. Two such myths are especially popular in our own day—that tradition is a bond transforming society into community, and that it is only large societies, not societies in their very nature, that are antithetical to community.

The idealization of tradition is the work primarily of conservatives.

Resisting the revolutionary impulses of the modern era, conservatives have argued, often eloquently, that the tension between social unity and individual personality exists mainly where social unity is a product of conscious design. That tension would be largely resolved if society were preserved from generation to generation and were cared for as a precious inheritance and not merely as a mechanism for serving economic and military needs. Framed in ancient traditions rather than in governmental decrees, human relationships would be communal; and they would unify, in their communality, not only the living but the dead and the unborn as well.

It cannot be denied that this vision contains some truth. Traditions may mitigate the expediential harshness of society and may provide gratifying and salutary reminders of the past. And old institutions may represent an accumulation of prudent adjustments that cannot be reduced to any rational formula and cannot be readily replaced. Is it not clear, however, that when conservative counsel is consistently followed what is saved are for the most part relics of past economic and military necessities? Is it not also clear that these relics continue to serve functions of organization and appraisal, if only by lending the social order a mollifying charm and splendor?

If the key to community for some is tradition, for others it is smallness. Societies supposedly are impersonal and anticommunal not in essence but only because of their excessive size. If all could participate directly in public business, hierarchies of organization and appraisal would give way to democratic, inquiring assemblies. This view draws sustenance both from the persistently alien and desolate character of contemporary industrial society and from the romantic image of the city-states of ancient Greece. Rousseau, inspired by Sparta, expressed his feeling for small societies when he pointed to the immensity of the nations of his time as "the first and principal source of the woes of the human race," and asserted that "almost all small states, Republics and Monarchies alike, prosper due to the fact alone that they are small."[3]

A society much smaller than a nation-state, however, would either

3. Jean Jacques Rousseau, *Considérations sur le Gouvernement de Pologne*, in *The Political Writings of Jean Jacques Rousseau*, ed. C. E. Vaughan (2 vols.; New York: John Wiley, 1962), II, 442 (my translation).

be too small to be militarily defensible and economically efficient; or it would be too large (even if it were relatively small, like an American state) to be a truly personal association; and it might be both. The ancient Greek city-states exemplify this assertion. Even in an age of primitive technology, they were not in the long run militarily defensible, as is proven by their inability to remain independent of Macedonia or Rome. Also, it is plain that a society as small as ancient Athens or Sparta would be incapable of the extensive specialization and domestic trade on which highly developed industrialism depends.

Further, a small society must have fewer spiritual resources—creative individuals, schools of thought, and the like—than a large society. We forget this mainly because of our consciousness of the cultural riches that poured out of ancient Athens. But Athens was altogether exceptional, not merely in history broadly, but even in ancient Greece. It is reasonable to suppose that life in Thebes or Megara, not to speak of any of the dozens of lesser cities, was often spiritually stultifying.

Yet, while the Greek city-states were too small in some ways, they were not small enough to be bound together by personal relationships. Rousseau cites first among the advantages of smallness that "all citizens are mutually acquainted." But even in a city with only a thousand citizens all could not be mutually acquainted, and cities in Greece ordinarily contained many thousands of citizens. In view of the depersonalization entailed both by numbers and by the intrinsic purposes of society, it is not surprising to find that the Greek city-states were far from purely personal associations. Many of them were rigidly controlled oligarchies on the pattern of Sparta; some were tyrannies. As for the democracies, aside from the exclusion from citizenship of most of the adult inhabitants, accounts of clamorous assemblies and ascendant demagogues show that even among the citizens popular rule did not eliminate depersonalization and domination.

We have now reached a favorable position for reflecting on equality. The ideal of equality, as I have said, is not wrong. It is perhaps as nearly right as any ideal can be. Partly for this very reason, however, it lends great force to the destructive notion that in one particular form of society lies community.

Equality and Community

Since as early as 1776 Western man has been engaged in a great struggle over the issue of equality.[4] A struggle of this kind can of course be seen in most periods of history—in ancient Greece and Rome, for example. Starting with the American and French Revolutions, however, the idea of equality has occasioned a conflict more ideological and more global than any of the earlier struggles. At first, equality was opposed primarily by the landed aristocracy. As industrialism developed, however, the middle classes that had led the crusade for equality joined, and in some measure replaced, the aristocracy. The idea of equality came to be championed mainly by middle-class intellectuals speaking in behalf of the lower classes. All along, however, the general issue has remained the same.

In my opinion, one should not try to stand above this conflict, asserting that both sides are partly right and partly wrong. The truth is that the ideal of equality expresses more fully and unambiguously than the opposing principle the major moral intuition of the West, the dignity of every human being. Hence if it were necessary to oversimplify so drastically as to say that one side is right and one side wrong, it would have to be said that the side of equality is right. Equal dignity is of course not the same as equal intelligence or equal experience; it does not preclude recognition of empirical inequalities. It does, however, relativize such inequalities, implying that they do not pertain to the very essence of man and thus do not have the moral importance often attributed to them.

The moral primacy of the principle of equality is indicated by its link with the ideal of community. Love is all-inclusive and man therefore comes to envision, as is seen in the history both of Judeo-Christian thought and of Greek philosophy, not only the unity of mankind but the abolition of all rank and privilege. In the activity of communication, love becomes a will to include all without exception in a single sphere of discourse—a sphere in which all are accorded attention, all addressed. The appearance of inferiority and superiority checks this will. The

4. See R. R. Palmer, *The Age of Democratic Revolution: A Political History of Europe and America, 1760–1800* (2 vols.; Princeton: Princeton University Press, 1959).

necessity for recognizing gradations of intelligence and insight is experienced as an intrusion of objectification, of appraisal, into an intersubjective realm. Communal man is egalitarian.

The very meaning of equality is best put in terms of community. To enjoy equality is not just to occupy the same social and economic level as everyone else, although that may be part of it. It is to be addressed and listened to in matters of the greatest moment. I am not accorded dignity by someone who feeds me but does not care what I think. Even animals may be given food and shelter; the decisive signs of respect are serious listening and speaking. The dignity of a person consists in the right fully to participate in the search for truth.

Morally, then, the ideal of equality is uniquely compelling. Practically, however, it is subject to serious doubts. It renders the will to unity powerful but indiscriminate and often enhances the anticommunal character of society.

For one thing, it is usually difficult, and sometimes impossible, to give equality any practical definition except uniformity. All must have incomes of the same amount, clothing and housing of the same quality, education of the same excellence. To be sure, it is easy to speak of diversities that imply no inequalities. The same income may be spent in various ways, clothing and housing alike in quality may differ in style, and two people may be equally well educated although coming from very dissimilar schools. In practice, however, diversities invite invidious comparisons. Moreover, diversities are not easily provided for great numbers of people; a large measure of standardization, whether in material goods or in spiritual matters such as education, seems inescapable. Hence the phenomenon of "the masses."

Further, a crusade for equality is apt to result in new inequalities. Those who promote equality with greatest determination do not simply destroy the old rulers and reigning classes; they replace them. All others, having lost traditional rank and privileges—even the privileges associated with very low rank—become merely objects for organization and appraisal. However unexpected this development has been, the reasons behind it are clear in the light of the preceding discussion. It is impossible wholly to divest society of hierarchies of organization and appraisal. Hence, if these are done away with in one form they necessarily reappear in another. If they are done away with by people who anticipate the dawn of full equality and thus make no provision for keeping power limited and responsible, they may reappear in forms more inhumane than those of the past. Thus the doctrine of equality, stimulating unguarded hope, may enhance the force and harshness of inequality. This explains in part what has happened in the Soviet Union. Ancient hierarchies have been replaced by those of government and party, and inequality is not less drastic and morally questionable than it was a century ago under the czars.

In sum, equality as a moral principle is nearly irresistible but as a practical maxim undergoes a strange reversal of meaning. Asserting the dignity of each person, it tends to submerge the person in a remorselessly unified society. Attacking all rank and privilege, it calls forth new forms of domination.

Radicals are apt to view such statements with impatience and suspicion. For all practical purposes, they equate equality and community, assuming that opposition to the former is opposition to the latter as well—probably in defense of property or privilege. Radical *philosophy* is not usually so indiscriminate, but radical *propaganda* usually is. Like those whom Dostoevsky foresaw raising a banner reading, "Feed men, then ask of them virtue," radical polemicists typically demand that we equalize men, then seek community—assuming that once equality has been achieved, community will be near at hand.[5]

The dubiousness of this assumption, however, is indicated by our experience of mass society. It is true that nothing like full equality has been attained anywhere. In America there is a large impoverished minority and within the prosperous majority there are widely varying degrees of prosperity. Nevertheless, much equalization has occurred. In a number of the Western industrial nations, a large middle class enjoys material conveniences and comforts inaccessible to kings in earlier ages and lives roughly in the same fashion, although not as securely, as do the wealthiest classes. Yet as this mass equality has grown, so, it seems, has alienation—judging, at least, by indices such as spreading bureaucracy and increasing mobility and by works of literature and sociological analysis. Drawing nearer to equality, we have seen community recede.

It does not appear that we can ignore community pending the estab-

5. Fyodor Dostoevsky, *The Brothers Karamazov*, trans. Constance Garnett (New York: Modern Library, no date), 262.

lishment of equality. By concentrating exclusively on equality we risk falling into a new barbarism, inherent in the unprecedented degree of social unity made possible by modern technology, and no less destructive for matching the demands of equal justice. The signal defect of radicalism is that it encourages, even insists upon, this perilous one-sidedness.

Many radicals today, of course, vigorously condemn Stalinist bureaucracy and search for more communal ways of organizing industrial society, for ways of achieving equality without depersonalization. It would exhibit a doctrinaire pessimism not to admit that they may uncover valuable possibilities of social reorganization. But often they seem to assume that society can be fully communal, and that it is necessary only for it to be organized in the right way, by the right people. In this way their research supports dangerous illusions. It is not surprising that some people have turned emphatically away from radicalism and the radical axiom of equality.

Inequality and Community

It is not in lacking substantial principles to stand on that defenders of inequality are wrong. It is in their manner of asserting these principles—in holding, as they often do, that some hierarchical system, either one inherited or one that could be established, provides a fully satisfactory way of organizing society. In this way, like their radical opponents, they deny the principle of plurality and enfold some particular order of society in a delusory aura of community. Let us first look at their principles.

The argument for inequality is particularly strong if it is stated as a matter of practicality. However equal people may be in ultimate dignity, they are not equal in practical ability and society cannot work without allotting responsibilities that both command and deserve differing degrees of respect. The argument that such inequalities of ability and function exist whether we approve of them or not, and that society cannot with impunity ignore them, is compelling.

The argument for inequality does not derive its strength from practical considerations alone, however. In most forms that argument is an implicit repudiation of the relativism that makes it impossible to differentiate truly great achievements from things someone merely happens to like. To distinguish superior from ordinary human beings is to affirm standards of excellence—artistic, political, and so forth. The doctrine of equality, on the other hand, tempts us to abandon such standards. If value is identical with preference, then we need not doubt that all are equal. Nor need we become involved in paradoxical tasks such as that of distributing power unequally among those whom we consider to be equal in dignity. The defense of inequality is, at its best, a defense of civilization against anomic, barbarizing egalitarianism.

Defenders of inequality thus can claim to be both realistic and principled. They often wish to go further, however, and to assert that some known, or as yet unknown but knowable, system of ranking human beings is absolutely just. They are not willing to say merely that inequalities of rank are necessary, however questionable; they wish to say that some particular rule of precedence, founded perhaps on philosophical wisdom, as in Plato, or on possession of inherited land, is absolutely just. Like radicals, they wish to place society under the governance of a single principle.

But human beings are not subject to the assured and comprehensive judgment that would be necessary if this were to be done. The reason is partly that our ability to judge one another and to distinguish the excellent from the mediocre is slight. This is true even within particular fields, like art, scholarship, or politics. We can see that some seem to have done better at certain tasks than others, but we cannot reliably generalize. When we try to designate the better artists, the better scholars, the better leaders, we know that our judgments may legitimately be contested and that we ourselves may in time revise them. When we try to generalize more broadly we are certain to fail. Some excel in one respect and some in another; none excel in every respect. Even if we can tell which are the better artists, scholars, and leaders, we cannot tell which are the better human beings.

The heart of the difficulty is that man's various qualities do not add up to a totality that even in principle is accessible to judgment. This is shown in Kant's *Critique of Pure Reason*. In some aspects, of course, man can be known, as he is in the social sciences. As a whole, however, a person is not and will never be merely an object of knowledge and judgment; indeed, as Kant shows, he is not even the kind of being to whom a phrase like "on the whole" can be appropriately applied. Here we come close to the insight underlying the ideal of equality. Judging and ranking are tragic necessities not just because in carrying them out we are apt to err; they violate the mystery of man.

Along with such theoretical considerations, we must not fail to note a practical consideration as well. High rank is often morally damaging. Power and status do not invariably corrupt those enjoying them, but they do so often enough to warrant a certain suspicion of people in the highest positions of power and honor. Ironically, many such people may be found who do not deserve their positions primarily because of the effects of their having them.

If inequality were the sole standard of social and political organization, community would be crushed by society. This would happen with any conception of inequality whatever, whether based on education, on property, or on any other sign of excellence. The effects would be similar to those of making equality the supreme and solitary standard. Society would become more dangerous, for awareness of its inherent imperfection would give way to an ideal of perfect order. In addition, a few would be vested with unwarrantable powers of organization and appraisal—unwarrantable because they would be accorded under the guidance of a conviction no less illusory than the egalitarian expectation that the functions of organization and appraisal will wither away: the conviction that those absolutely best fitted for organizing and appraising their fellow beings can be assuredly identified and empowered. In short, if inequality were the sole standard of organization, it would produce not community but mere unity.

The Wisdom of Indecision

The main conclusion to which we are led, I suggest, is that the issue of equality *versus* inequality is irresolvable. It may be compromised, on the basis of an intuitive sense of the necessities of the moment, but not subsumed under a more comprehensive principle. There is no escaping the competing imperatives of moral equality and empirical inequality.

To someone in a mood of philosophical detachment, such a conclusion may seem sensible. But human beings generally are not very philosophical or detached, and in many cases economic deprivation renders such attitudes so difficult as to seem inappropriate. Hence the world as a whole and almost every society is divided between those committed, under one formula or another, either to equality or to inequality. Many are willing to compromise temporarily, but few are willing to think that compromise is not only practically necessary but morally obligatory and that this will be so for as long as history continues.

Some have tried to resolve the conflict by distinguishing between equality of opportunity and what they refer to as "equality of result." As a rough practical maxim perhaps that distinction is of some use. For devising a concept of justice, however, it is without value. That a fair ranking of persons requires equality of opportunity goes without saying. But the most perfect equality of opportunity would not eliminate the conjectural, relative, and unstable character of the inequalities resulting. Further, complete equality of opportunity would be impossible without something at least very close to complete equality of result. It is difficult to think of any inequality of result—power? social status? income?—that does not entail inequality of opportunity. The complete inadequacy of this popular formula indicates the inextinguishable character of the issue it is supposed to resolve.

If there is no concept of justice that will reconcile equality and inequality, then we are brought back to the principle of plurality. The principle that bars unqualified adherence to any single rule of social and political organization never had a more fitting application than to the issue that has so divided mankind since 1776. To be consistently egalitarian or inegalitarian is possible only on the premise that the defects of society are only accidental. The result of such consistency is apt to be either a pseudoprogressive bureaucracy or a neotribal cult of leadership. Both have been seen in our time and both foreclose the possibility of community.

It is natural for us, as rational beings, to want our political principles to be worked out logically and applied unrestrictedly. Thus in the conflict between equality and inequality, some demand pure democracy in all spheres—in politics, in industry, in culture—while others are convinced that human affairs will be in disarray until the best and the most powerful among men are the same. The crux of the conclusion to which these reflections have brought us is that it is dangerous to be so logical.

Realizing the inherent impossibility of converting society into community has never been more important than it is today, for society has never been more omnipresent and overbearing. Industrial technology has provided the material basis for unification, such as standardized products, media for instant and global communication, and instruments of surveillance. Refined techniques of organization and appraisal, like those used in factories and office staffs, have enabled institutions to become larger and more cohesive. The doctrine of equality seems to have done less to protect people in these circumstances than it has, by weakening traditional distinctions and privileges, to increase their vulnerability to them.

The alienation that is so prevalent a theme of contemporary social criticism can be understood from this standpoint. This alienation is not, according to most descriptions, anything so traditional and limited as mere loneliness. Its mood is one of totality. The individual feels estranged from all human beings, from all reality, even from himself. This is readily explained if it is society as a systematic and all-inclusive totality from which the individual is estranged. What makes all human beings and all reality seem alien is their absorption within a single organized order. The fact that society may not be outwardly oppressive, but mild and benign (as industrial wealth makes it possible for it to be), enhances the poignancy of alienation. With ostensible happiness all about him, the alienated individual is deprived not only of community but also of obvious grievances. He may feel not only desolate but guilty.

The most extreme point ever reached in the unification of society is represented by twentieth-century totalitarianism. Every person is totally mobilized; appraisal is all-pervasive; the supreme organizers and appraisers are human gods. Although often lurid and grotesque, totalitarianism is not just an aberration. Its exaggerations reveal the enduring characteristics of society. In addition, they enable us to mark the direction in which we have been moving: toward a fatal confusion of society and community.

It would be far too simple to say that equality has been the main motive in the aggrandizement of society. But equality has reinforced that trend with a powerful moral ideal. That egalitarianism, outwardly so right-minded, can lead even to the social and political enormity of totalitarianism is clearly written in the history of the Soviet Union. Purely Russian conditions played a role, to be sure, but that role was shaped by an intense moral consciousness. Egalitarianism is dangerous because it has a moral authority that makes for fanaticism. It is dangerous because it is right.

Hence one should not try to face radicals and their egalitarian demands with an easy conscience or an invariable rule of conduct. What right have we to delay in rectifying wrongs suffered by others? None that can be found in pure moral doctrine. But along with morals, circumstances also count for something, and these repeatedly create a burden of uneasiness and indecision. To accept this burden, and with it the guilt of temporizing with injustice, is the destiny of a communal being in a universe that offers only fragmentary and ephemeral experiences of community.

V / IN DEFENSE OF PURE TOLERANCE

Tolerance is one of the most dubitable of all virtues. Where it is not repudiated and crushed altogether, it is probably normal for it to be under attack. It is apt to be a source of annoyance, if not genuine trouble, and the arguments supporting it are often paradoxical and complex. It is quite possible for a reasonable person to be intolerant. The ideal of tolerance arose, in the sixteenth and seventeenth centuries, not so much because tolerance seemed to be good in itself as because it seemed to be the only alternative to endless religious wars. For many, it was a necessary evil.

Troublesome in practice and merely expediential in its origins, tolerance is a weak ideal. The liberal individualism on which it is ordinarily based does little to overcome its weakness. An individual fundamentally detached from all other individuals—the primary concept of traditional liberalism—may be unconcerned, and thus not disposed to interfere, with the beliefs of others. He would therefore ordinarily be tolerant, but for no better reason than indifference. His tolerance would consequently be wholly dependent on circumstances and would lack any moral grounds of its own. It would not be pure—giving the word *pure* a meaning analogous to that which Kant gave it in his First Critique, a meaning presupposed in the title of a well-known contemporary work on tolerance, *A Critique of Pure Tolerance*.[1] Liberal tolerance is impure by being contingent on empirical conditions.

This suggests that replacing the ideal of individual self-sufficiency with that of community might provide the basis for a stronger doctrine of tolerance, a doctrine that would construe tolerance as a positive

1. Robert Paul Wolff, Barrington Moore, Jr., and Herbert Marcuse, *A Critique of Pure Tolerance* (Boston: Beacon Press, 1965).

human relationship and not merely as an expression of indifference; a doctrine that would place tolerance among the principal standards of civility; above all, a doctrine that would interpret tolerance as a moral imperative, and thus as an imperative not dependent wholly on circumstances for its validity. The question on which we shall reflect, then, is whether our communality does not point toward a purer—a less expediential and more principled—tolerance than is traditional in the liberal democracies.

To pursue this question means entertaining the possibility of a new philosophical alliance. Traditionally, while individualism has provided the philosophical grounds for tolerance, the ideal of community has been allied with a belief in social solidarity that allowed little room for tolerance. Thus the classical case for tolerance was made by two radical individualists, John Locke and John Stuart Mill. The great defenders of community, such as Rousseau and Hegel, were either opposed to tolerance or had little to say in its favor. These connections are discernible in our own time. Tolerance is supported mainly by liberals who argue that each one has a right to his own thoughts and his own mode of life. Intolerance is most evident among radicals, who reject individualism and extol community, and among conservative patriots who speak for the solidarity of the nation. This connection must be broken if tolerance is to be placed on communal grounds.

The possibility of forging a new alliance, however, depends on a different, and truer, concept of community than any ordinarily held on the left or the right. The effort to outline such a concept was made in the course of the preceding reflections, especially in Chapter II, where it is proposed that community consists in communication. Community, it may be said, is enacted in the activity of communication. It might be well for us to recall that concept; then perhaps we can see whether it provides a better basis for tolerance than does individualism.

Community, Communication, and Truth

It is strange that communication has been so little thought of in connection with community. Rousseau's *Social Contract* is probably the major classic of modern times concerning community, yet there is practically nothing in it concerning communication. Communism and socialism are movements seeking to establish community on the foundations provided by industrialism, yet communist and socialist writers have little to say about communication. Karl Marx, to my knowledge, never devoted any sustained attention to the subject. At present, the most outspoken defenders of community are radical young people and conservative nationalists; neither show much interest in communication. Thus the concepts of community and communication seem to have fallen into separate spheres of discourse.

Such a split is illogical and destructive. Community comes to be conceived of as something static and unfree. Communication, separated from the noble and comprehensive ideal of community, is identified with such activities as advertising or merely transmitting information. Community and communication were at one in two of the greatest figures of ancient thought, Plato and Augustine, and the recovery of this unity may be seen as one of the major responsibilities of social and political thought today.

For any such recovery to be significant, however, we have to remember what communication is. We have to remember a central theme of Chapter II—that communication is in the nature of inquiry. It is an exploratory enterprise undertaken in the company of others. This is to say that it is concerned with truth and that mere persuasion, without regard for the truth, is not necessarily communication at all. It is to say also that it is concerned with truth that is not possessed but transcends every explicit conclusion; hence merely transmitting what is already securely known is communication only in a relatively trivial sense. Corresponding with this conception of communication, community is not in the nature of an order that is changeless and that members must simply accept or quit. Community must be unsettled and must call upon the creative resources of its participants.

These assertions, although contrary to prevailing assumptions, can be derived from views of community that almost everyone holds. For example, communication and community are presumably matters of sharing. But where an untruth is told there is no sharing at all, and where mere information is transmitted, relatively little is shared. Serious sharing is inseparable from an orientation toward ultimate being, toward truth in the fullest sense. But truth must transcend the content of any particular communication; therefore involvement in communication presupposes an exploratory attitude, a disposition to question and to search. It follows that people who share only an unquestioned dogma, or an all-absorbing emotional state, do not constitute a community.

Presumably community brings people together in their essential being. This is another view of community that almost everyone would accept. Yet people do not realize their essential being by suppressing their critical powers. On the contrary, if man is essentially rational then he is essentially a critical and questioning creature. True communication is exemplified in the life of Socrates, who presented himself in his full humanity as one bound to enter into rational inquiry with his friends and fellow citizens.

The way we have trivialized and twisted the concept of community betrays our preoccupation with activities such as advertising, electioneering, and entertainment. We have forgotten that human beings are genuinely united only so far as they are united by things that really are—not by illusions and lies—and by the most important things that are—not by matters that can be reduced to factual information. We have forgotten, in other words, that human beings are united only by the truth and that the truth is something we search for and do not securely possess. We remind ourselves of these things, and of their meaning for human relations, when we say that community is that which comes to pass through serious communication.

It must be admitted that we thus involve ourselves in conceptual difficulties. Our minds deal easily and naturally with physical realities but only haltingly and painfully with spiritual realities. Hence we tend to think of community as analogous to a physical structure, such as a house. When a house is being built, we think of the house as not yet real; it becomes real only when it is finished. With community, the case is just the opposite. It is real only while communication is being carried on; once communication ceases then community is no longer a present reality. Community is inherently unfinished. It is not the product of the activity but is the activity itself. But how is this conceivable? How can anything real be "inherently unfinished"? How can community be the good that man seeks if community is inquiry and inquiry is the search for a good that he lacks?

Although standard logic is a source of serious difficulty for the idea of community that I suggest, there is another, more human logic. It is reflected in Gotthold Ephraim Lessing's well-known statement that if God held the truth in one hand and the eternal search for the truth in the other and commanded him to choose, he would choose the eternal search. It is the logic of Lessing, I think, that must govern us in trying to understand community.

Having in mind what community is and why we care about it, let us explore the possibility of reinterpreting tolerance as a communal, rather than an individualistic virtue.

Community and Tolerance

The relationship between community and tolerance depends partly on how and when community can be realized in history. Two assumptions in this regard are particularly common among proponents of community. One is that community can be assured through action, through certain definite steps, either known or discoverable. The other assumption is that these steps will soon be taken and that community is therefore historically imminent; communal man does not have long to wait. Both of these assumptions are illustrated in Marxism, where the ideal of community is imbued with confidence alike in action and in the impending future.

These assumptions cut the roots of tolerance and help to explain the frequent conflict between community and tolerance. A conception of community as something that can be created leaves no room for tolerance. Not only is tolerance unnecessary as a condition of community but it may stand in the way of actions leading to community. Moreover, if we are soon to enter into community and thus be at one, why should we subject ourselves to the unpleasant demands of tolerance? We inhabit a brief transitional period and soon all need for tolerance will have passed.

If the ideal of tolerance is to be based on that of community, these assumptions must be rejected. Can that be legitimately done? That it can with the first assumption is implied by the preceding reflections. As we have already seen, if community arises from communication, it cannot possibly be an object of action. Communication in its nature is free, whereas action is an application of power. Conditions favoring community might be created through action, but the link between these conditions and community itself cannot be conceived of as causally necessary without denying the freedom that belongs to the essence of communication. If a community were merely some solidified social grouping, then it might be created through action—probably through intolerant action, such as the expulsion of poets from Plato's ideal republic. Some political philosophers have conceived of communal life as conformity with an ideal order rather than as communication; thus for Rousseau and Hegel community membership meant above all obedience to the law. From this standpoint it is not difficult to envision community as a product of action. From the standpoint of preceding reflections, however, nothing that is a product of action could be a community.

As for the second assumption—that community, somewhere or everywhere, soon will be realized—there is at the very least much room for doubt. Little either in the historical trends of our time or in man's nature as disclosed in literary introspection, scientific investigation, and historical research renders community in any full measure, in any nation and in the foreseeable future, a reasonable expectation. Faith in a coming transformation of man and his life cannot be absolutely barred, but neither can it be supported by empirical evidence. The realistic prospect before us is that of a world in which community is fragmentary and evanescent, a world in which no nation or polity is concerned consistently and effectively enough with communication to be counted as a community.

In sum, the realities of the historical world do not accord with our communal nature. We cannot alter this situation by action, and there is no reason to expect the situation to change spontaneously. This does not leave us altogether confined, however, to the beleaguered communal redoubts that take shape here and there in the world. I suggest that a person can place himself in a kind of communal relationship with mankind even where there is no community, and that this is done through tolerance. This may best be understood by taking note of a concept worked out by Martin Buber.

Buber spent a great part of his life reflecting on community. In one of his last works he discussed what he called "primal setting at a distance." This, according to Buber, is presupposed in every act of communication. "One can enter into relation only with being which has been set at a distance," Buber argued.[2] Broadening this proposition into an anthropological principle, he asserted that "man, as man, sets man at a distance and makes him independent; he lets the life of men like himself go on round about him, and so he, and he alone, is able to enter into relation, in his own individual status, with those like himself."[3]

Buber does not explicitly mention tolerance, but is this not what he is speaking of? Not, of course, if tolerance is understood negatively, so that it connotes indifference rather than attentiveness, and mere separateness rather than readiness for communication. But it is not apparent why tolerance should be understood in this way or how it can be a human relationship, and thus a moral obligation, if it is. If man is a communal being, tolerance must be envisioned instead as recognition that the other is a being like oneself, who can speak and listen, and who needs freedom to do either one authentically. If tolerance is envisioned in this way, it may be said to constitute communal space, interpersonal room in which communication is possible. One who is tolerated is allowed to remain at a distance, but not at a distance that is untraversable.

If we keep strictly to the limits of Buber's analysis, tolerance is precommunal. To address or accord attention to someone, I must first (logically, not temporally) have recognized him as the kind of being with whom such relations are appropriate, and in doing this I must have granted him the interpersonal space that communication requires. The principle of life, for Buber, is a "two-fold movement"—setting at a distance and entering into relations. We may interpret tolerance as being the first of these movements. The idea that tolerance is an indispensable precommunal movement accords logically with a conclusion reached earlier in these reflections: community cannot be a product of action.

Moving slightly beyond the limits of Buber's analysis, however, can deepen our appreciation of tolerance. Buber was decidedly optimistic and saw community as readily accessible; consequently he saw "primal setting at a distance"—in our terms, tolerance—as only a temporary state, a preparatory act that would be fulfilled in communication. But

2. Martin Buber, *The Knowledge of Man: Selected Essays*, ed. Maurice Friedman; trans. Maurice Friedman and Ronald Gregor Smith (New York: Harper & Row, 1965), 60.
    3. *Ibid.*, 67.

what is the significance of this act if it is rarely fulfilled, if communication is a difficult and rare achievement? I suggest that it does not lose, but gains in significance. It becomes apparent that what Buber saw as only a *pre*communal state is in itself a partial realization of community. It is, so to speak, a *semi*communal state. The distance established by tolerance is not an alienating distance. Thus although those who merely tolerate one another do not make up a community, neither are they simply estranged. Tolerance is the bond of a pessimist's community: the relationships it entails are tenuous in comparison with those envisioned by the great proponents of community, such as Plato and Buber, but they are far more substantial than the relations of mutual indifference or controlled hostility that have been acceptable to individualists such as Locke and Hobbes.

The standard of tolerance calls for a kind of communal modesty. The very validity of the ideal of community helps to give it a compelling power over human imagination and to call forth oversimplified and distorted concepts of community. Both fascism and Soviet communism are examples. If community is to be widely sought, it would be well for this to be done soberly, on the basis of accurate conceptions of the nature and requirements of community. Rightly understood, tolerance is an ideal calculated to check thoughtless communal enthusiasm. What it does is to require, before communal dreams are enacted, a prior step: the granting of distance. Much misery might have been avoided had man, in his passion for community, always been cognizant of the need for this first step.

But here we must concern ourselves primarily with theoretical, rather than practical, implications. What has been said so far is a very incomplete defense of tolerance, for little account has been taken of the arguments against it. Faced with such arguments, is communal tolerance more defensible than individualistic tolerance?

The burden of many, perhaps most, arguments against tolerance is not that tolerance is inherently evil (even so dogmatic a thinker as Augustine did not believe this) but that it impedes the realization of some greater value. Thus, for example, Plato seems to have been intolerant primarily because he thought that tolerance would stand in the way of achieving justice. Augustine reluctantly endorsed the forcible suppression of heresy when he became convinced that the health of Christianity would otherwise be endangered. What we must consider, therefore, is the relationship of tolerance to values other than community.

Tolerance and the Good

The classical theory of tolerance, as set forth by Locke and Mill, tended to ignore the possibility that some of the most important values are discordant—that liberty, for example, may undermine justice, or equality clash with culture. The prospects of serious moral conflict were minimized. As a result, tolerance was presented as a policy without grave risks or drawbacks, as wholly advantageous. Is such an attitude justified?

Surely it is not. Historical reality is too complex and treacherous to provide assurance that every important value will be furthered by, or is even compatible with, tolerance. This can be seen in relation to several major values.

1. *Justice*. In the United States, where tolerance is as broad and reliable as anywhere on earth, there is apparently a widespread willingness to accept the indefinite continuation of drastic economic inequalities and racial injustices. Granted, it is not perfectly clear what should be done about these conditions; what concerns us here is that the majority does not seem greatly to care. This suggests that Plato's opposition to tolerance was not mistaken. Where all can think and speak as they like, true standards of justice are likely to be submerged under public indifference and confusion. In Plato's ideal state, under the absolute rule of philosophers, such attitudes would neither be so likely to prevail nor would they be so decisive in the governance of the state.

2. *Order*. One of Locke's most emphatic arguments in favor of tolerance was that it tends to quench sedition and give rise to order. In some circumstances, probably it would—where, for example, a particular minority is convinced that it will be destroyed unless it overthrows the government and seizes power itself. But the twentieth century has had too much experience with fanaticism of a kind that gains virulence with power for Locke's argument to stand as a general rule. Does not the fate of Weimar Germany, destroyed by a minority that took advantage of tolerance to create a public atmosphere of hatred

and fear, demonstrate the possible discordance between tolerance and order?

3. *Democracy*. Tolerance is not reliably in harmony with popular rule because it necessarily provides opportunities for privileged minorities to gain disproportionate power. It is the gist of Marxism that this necessarily happens in capitalist systems. The major founder of the democratic ideal, Rousseau, feared minorities to such an extent that his own model of democracy may fairly be called an intolerant, even totalitarian, democracy.

4. *Happiness*. Tolerance must be ineffective if it does not often give rise to unwelcome doubts. One might properly be contemptuous of a society so uniformly complacent that tolerance would disturb no one's peace of mind. Thus the utilitarian defense—linking tolerance with happiness—is questionable. Dostoevsky was probably nearer the truth. He argued that if the end is happiness, what is needed, rather than freedom, is "bread, miracles, and authority."

In short, it is reasonable to think that tolerance is dangerous. It is scarcely realistic to think that any policy will be attended only with advantages; it would be particularly unrealistic to think this of tolerance—a policy, as Ortega puts it, of sharing existence with the enemy.[4] How seriously is tolerance compromised by the admission that it may endanger values as fundamental as justice, order, democracy, and happiness?

First of all, since we are trying here to be realistic, it must be noted that the counsels of realism are not wholly antithetical to tolerance. A realist might observe, for example, that not only tolerance, but also the absence of tolerance, is dangerous. The absence of tolerance implies concentrated power, and that is not a circumstance favorable to values such as justice and happiness. Indeed, most people would assume that an absolute government is the most dangerous of regimes. Thus tolerance may be defended not as an ideal arrangement but merely as one that in most circumstances is preferable to alternative arrangements.

A realist might also draw attention to the possibility of reducing the risks of tolerance through political prudence. It is striking how little is said about politics in the classical works on tolerance. There is little

4. José Ortega y Gasset, *The Revolt of the Masses* (New York: W. W. Norton, 1932), 76. His exact words are: "Liberalism . . . announces determination to share existence with the enemy."

exaggeration in saying that Locke and Mill regarded tolerance as a substitute for politics. They saw tolerance as making so powerfully for social harmony that the scope of political artifice would be greatly reduced. Neither thinker manifests any clear awareness that tolerance may create political problems. That it may, however, is implicit in the acknowledgment that tolerance may come into conflict with other values. The point a realist might make is that such conflict need not be unmanageable. In contrast with the apolitical character of the liberal theory of tolerance, a realistic tolerance would be informed with a Machiavellian sense that freedom does not eliminate but rather places demands on political art.

The fundamental response that must be made in behalf of tolerance, however, does not concern its practicality but rather its value: it is so crucial to human relations that the risks it involves must be taken. This is implicit in the idea that man is a communal being and that only through tolerance does he bear himself as such.

Applying this principle to the values with which tolerance comes into conflict, it may be said that what tolerance does in relation to every value is to establish a "margin of communality." By this I mean that it bars any value from being a mere dogma or command; it exposes every value to criticism and inquiry. In this way it creates a possibility that the good will be a matter of communication and common understanding, adhered to freely. This cannot be done without risks; something of worth may be attacked and defeated. But if it is not done at all, then values lose their moral significance. They become grounds and pretexts for despotism rather than genuine human needs. This can be seen in connection with each of the points discussed above.

1. No one concerned with justice can be satisfied with just behavior that is exacted by force or by "noble lies." Justice sometimes must be imposed; but the ideal of justice is surely that there should be just human beings and just human relationships, and these depend on conditions in which justice is consciously accepted and freely lived. It requires that justice be a matter of communal understanding. Plato, prescribing the enforcement of justice by absolute rulers, exemplifies the reluctance of morally serious people to risk the margin of communality. He exemplifies also the results of that reluctance—a political ideal in which only a tiny minority would be freely and thus genuinely just.

2. Order is perhaps the primary political demand; where it is lacking, little else can be achieved. Yet the mere absence of violence is not enough. Again and again it has been shown that people prefer chaos to some kinds of order. In certain circumstances tolerance may imperil order, but it also creates the possibility of order that is, if not just, at least commonly understood and freely accepted.

3. Democracy may mean either one of two very different things: that supreme power belongs to the people, or that the people are fully involved in the process of political deliberation. It may mean a system of rule or of universal communication. The two may of course be combined in various ways. The point regarding tolerance is that democracy as a system of rule is a species of political absolutism, as is shown in Hobbes' qualified approval of democracy, and that what saves it from being this is the margin of communality. It is through tolerance that the democratic process can become a means not just of marshalling majorities but of engaging in open political discourse.

4. Can happiness be legitimate if it is unshared and if it is unable to survive the threats to complacency that may arise where there is tolerance? There is a kind of happiness in which people are indifferent to one another and unconcerned with the issues of life. Such is the happiness depicted by Dostoevsky in the "Legend of the Grand Inquisitor"—a happiness that could not survive within a margin of communality. Tolerance opens the way—perhaps through suffering—to a happiness less fearful and less fragile.

In sum, if man is a communal being then nothing can be worthwhile that requires him to abandon the communal stance that is the essence of tolerance. Radical critics of tolerance, however, often hold that a communal stance is not enough, that achieving anything in the turbulence of actual life depends on certainty rather than the doubt encouraged by tolerance, and on readiness for action rather than the hesitancy apparently implicit in Buber's "primal setting at a distance." Let us consider these criticisms in turn.

Tolerance and Certainty

We are concerned with two different states. Certainty may characterize either a proposition or a state of mind. In one case it is objective, in the other subjective. Thus a proposition that can be scientifically demonstrated is objectively certain; on the other hand, if I adhere to a proposition without hesitation or doubt then I am subjectively certain even if the proposition happens to be demonstrably false. The objective and subjective states do not necessarily correspond. While a recognition of objective certainty must entail subjective certainty, the latter does not always or even usually wait upon the former.

The relationship of tolerance and objective certainty seems relatively simple. The burden of Barrington Moore's essay in the *Critique of Pure Tolerance* is that many questions dealt with both in the physical and social sciences can be conclusively settled; they need not, as proponents of tolerance sometimes encourage us to think, be everlastingly in doubt. This is a point that probably should be granted. It is true that there can be no absolute objective certainty concerning synthetic propositions. But to base tolerance on skepticism is a hazardous tactic. It is to place it in opposition both to common sense and to science, and it is also to invite an embarrassing rejoinder: if everything is in doubt, then so is tolerance.

Moreover, a skeptical defense of tolerance means giving up one of the strongest arguments in its favor—that it frees us for intellectual inquiry and in this way widens the areas of objective certainty. In short, tolerance increases knowledge. This was one of Mill's major arguments. It is not an invulnerable argument, as twentieth-century experience shows; dictatorships may vigorously advance scientific research. But it is a substantial argument. This can be seen in the Soviet support of geneticist Trofim Lysenko and the Nazi expulsion of Albert Einstein; dictatorial support of science is apt to be seriously affected by caprice or dogma. And it must be noted that the argument that tolerance favors objective certainty goes readily with a communal conception of tolerance, even though it was put forward by the individualistic Mill. It presupposes that tolerance opens the way to intellectual inquiry and offers in this way a communal opportunity.

The relationship of tolerance and the other type of certainty—*subjective* certainty—is a more controversial and difficult question. Some critics of tolerance, including Herbert Marcuse, charge that tolerance sanctions and encourages a state of political doubt and hesitancy that is not only epistemologically gratuitous but is socially harmful, since it induces people to acquiesce in injustice. Intolerant radicals have often felt that various wrongs within present society are perfectly obvious and that discussing them rather than simply fighting to suppress them, indulging thus in a state of subjective uncertainty, is temporizing with evils that are quite objective and quite certain.

It is indisputable that the practice of tolerance challenges every form of absolute assurance except that resting on scientifically demonstrable knowledge. Oliver Cromwell's moving injunction, "I beseech you, in the bowels of Christ, think it possible you may be mistaken," expresses, for anyone who would be tolerant, an ineluctable demand. One cannot accord attention to those he considers mistaken without entertaining the thought that perhaps he is the one who is mistaken. And this demand must have practical consequences. It would violate common sense to regard it as merely coincidental, for example, that American intellectual life today reflects broad tolerance and also, in religion and morals, pervasive doubt. Indeed, if tolerance were not accompanied by uncertainty of some kind and degree, one would suspect it of being a mere formality, without vital significance.

But tolerance does not necessarily engulf one in doubt. For one thing, in creating *objective* certainty it may create *subjective* certainty as well. This is what Mill had in mind when he defended tolerance on the grounds that it offers a way to "the intelligent and living apprehension" of the truth.[5] By taking in the reasons rendering a proposition objectively incontestable one gains inner assurance. In other words, only under the conditions established by tolerance can objective certainty be rationally recognized, and hence only under those conditions is *subjective* certainty, concerning matters of *objective* certainty, possible. But this brings us to an important question.

Can we reasonably anticipate, as Mill apparently did, that eventually all that man might desire to know will be known, and known as objectively certain? If so, then tolerance has a crucial role to play in the progress of civilization—but only temporarily. It establishes the intellectual medium in which we can come to comprehend ourselves and our circumstances scientifically; it is the way to an objective and subjec-

5. John Stuart Mill, *On Liberty*, in *Utilitarianism, Liberty, and Representative Government* (New York: E. P. Dutton, 1951), 138.

tive certainty embracing our relations with all realities. This is broadly Mill's defense of tolerance. It is a defense that can serve, however, only for a time. It reduces tolerance to a temporary expedient, the function of which will eventually be eliminated. Once comprehensive knowledge is achieved, tolerance has no further role of importance to play.

If tolerance is to be defended as having a place of permanent significance in civilized life, then the possibility of all reality being scientifically comprehended must be rejected. Limits must be placed on the possible scope of knowledge. The issue is, of course, too vast to be argued here. Hence I shall simply refer to an argument securely ranked among man's supreme philosophical achievements. In opposition to Mill I shall appeal to Kant.

It is a major theme of the *Critique of Pure Reason* that while a great deal of objectively certain knowledge can be gained, such knowledge is not and cannot be all-inclusive. The objective knowledge we possess is not just accidentally or temporarily incomplete. It is *essentially* incomplete, for being cannot be exhaustively objectified. It follows not only that the ultimate questions, such as the existence of God, cannot be objectively settled; even the ultimate significance of the objective certainties we do attain—of science and its conclusions—cannot be definitely known. We are, so to speak, encircled by uncertainty, and this situation will not be fundamentally altered by any accumulation of scientific knowledge.

But how does this view, assuming its validity, help the cause of tolerance? It may seem that the unknowability of being is no more favorable to tolerance than its knowability.

What needs to be noticed first is the possibility of attaining subjective certainty in the absence of objective certainty. Thus, for example, one may feel sure that it is man's obligation to seek justice for all even though he could not prove this to someone arguing that each person should take care solely of his own interests. It may seem that such inner assurance, in the absence of outer demonstrability, would be weak and unstable, liable to collapse in the face of threatened violence. But experience shows that this is not so. Practically every cause that human beings have ever died for—truth, freedom, justice, national independence—belongs among those matters concerning which no objective certainty is possible.

Man has a capacity, then, for an inner assurance that is independent of outer proof. What does tolerance have to do with this paradoxical state of mind? It is essential, I believe, for maintaining it in its full integrity. In refusing to impose my inner certainties on others I recognize that they are not outer certainties. By maintaining a tolerant relationship with others, I sustain an awareness of the character of my own loyalties. What particularly needs noting, however, is that this is important not just for others, who want to be free in their own loyalties; it is important for me as well. Here we come to one of the principal arguments in behalf of communal tolerance.

In leaving others free to reject my own deepest beliefs, I affirm and guard the integrity of those beliefs. I do this in two ways, first, by recognizing that they concern ultimate realities, not simply things that may be used, disposed of, or ignored. Such ideals as truth, freedom, and justice are not dignified when they are affirmed as matters of scientific certainty; on the contrary, they are degraded, for they are reduced to the level of the physical things all about us. Thus through tolerance I protect the dignity of the things I care most about. In addition to this, I protect my true relationship, which is one of freedom, with those things. Just as the highest ideals are not dignified by being asserted as matters of scientific knowledge, neither is man's relationship with those ideas strengthened if it is held that any reasonable person is bound by evidence and logic to accept them. Ultimate loyalties do not depend on intellectual compulsion but on a free orientation of one's whole being. A stance of communal tolerance, allowing others to turn away from realities I would very much like them to turn toward, recognizes this and keeps one from that tempting degradation of his loyalties that comes about when they are forced on others.

All of this points up the wisdom of one of the oldest and most frequently reiterated arguments for tolerance—that, after all, you may be wrong. You are not asked by those who employ this argument to give up your convictions, but only to recognize that they may be false. On the face of it, this is an absurd demand; to recognize that your convictions may be false is to begin to give them up. But we can see that the demand is not as absurd as it looks. Convictions are not necessarily destroyed or weakened by a realization of their objective uncertainty. Rather, they may be confirmed in their own distinctive nature as bonds with realities of another order than those within the scope of science, hence as cast in freedom rather than in logic.

We have here reached a position very much like that of Lessing when he chose the eternal search for truth in preference to the truth itself. And we can now see the reason for that choice. There is more truth in the eternal search than in a finished, securely possessed doctrine. This is hard for us to realize, but it is essential that we do so, for the sake not just of human decencies but of our apprehension of the truth. One of the greatest benefits of tolerance is that it continually forces us to recognize that ultimate realities are not like objects in the world, that ultimate truth is not scientifically demonstrable, and that the overall orientation of man in the universe is determined by freedom.

Such an attitude is highly paradoxical. Its validity, however, is indicated by its implicit presence in all philosophical reflection. Here it appears in two forms. First, to search for truth one must be capable of recognizing truth once it is found; but to do that one must in some sense already know the truth. This form of the paradox is seen most often, perhaps, in discussions concerning the relative priority of metaphysics and epistemology. It seems that one cannot arrive at metaphysical knowledge without having answered the epistemological question as to what knowledge is; but to answer that question seems to presuppose metaphysical knowledge.

The second form of the paradox is expressed in the age-old conception of philosophy as the love, not possession, of wisdom. The search for truth is endless. Just as searching for the truth depends on already, in some sense, knowing the truth, so knowing the truth depends on continuing to search for it. In these terms we may understand Socrates' profession that his wisdom consisted only in awareness of his ignorance.

Thus the divided mind presupposed by communal tolerance—subjective certainty, with objective uncertainty—is manifest not only in the heroism of those who have died in behalf of objectively questionable causes; it is as ancient and widespread as philosophy. It seems clear that tolerance does not necessarily leave men paralyzed by doubt. Not that it would never do this. Tolerance tends to make plain the limits of objective certainty, and it cannot be denied that for some—for all those mistaking faith for science—this will be a discouraging consequence. But it is apparent that discouragement of this sort originates in error. It is possible for man to live and even to die for the sake of the good without being under the illusion that his own conception of the good is in the nature of demonstrable truth. Socrates was not reduced to cowardice by his "ignorance."

To appreciate the nature, the strength, and the difficulty of the tolerant stance, however, it is essential to maintain its inner tension. This means on the one hand not letting go of the possibility of subjective certainty under the assumption that tolerance can remain afloat on a sea of all-engulfing doubt. Tolerance depends on assurance concerning several matters—concerning, for example, the dignity of persons and the value of truth. One who is uncertain of everything must be uncertain of the ideal of tolerance itself.

On the other hand, it is necessary to remember the objective uncertainties that encompass our certainties. We live, as it were, within two concentric spheres of being. Immediately around us lie the objective realities that are apprehended in experience and that evidence and logic force us to recognize. Tolerance within this sphere may provide a way to outer and inner certainty but is only a temporary expedient. The larger sphere is that of being itself, which is present to us in personal states of mind that cannot be scientifically validated—in love, in vision, in faith. The sphere of being itself is intimately personal, a sphere we inhabit by virtue not of intellectual necessity but of our ultimate loyalties and convictions. To mistake being itself for objective reality, the outer sphere for the inner, is so fundamental an error that it must be characterized as a kind of displacement in the cosmos, a loss of destiny. Thus keeping ourselves reminded of the objective uncertainty of our deepest beliefs is not imposing a deprivation on ourselves but is rather a way of guarding the integrity of our fundamental relationships.

In sum, we must strive for certainty but also for an understanding of the nature of our certainty. We do this through tolerance—tolerance understood, not in terms of individualism, but as a kind of communality. Thus understood, tolerance is a humane poise, a way of living with certitude that manifests itself as attentiveness and never as force.

All of these considerations together make for a complex and difficult argument. It cannot be claimed that the wisdom of communal tolerance is objectively certain. What can be claimed is that communal tolerance is a reasonable and civilized ideal. It recognizes that we are not compelled to be either filled with certainty or overwhelmed with uncertainty. We may not only know some things and doubt others but even somehow know and doubt the same things. Individualistic tolerance may well present simpler, less paradoxical demands; but these advantages are gained by abstracting man from mankind. The complexities and tensions of communal tolerance are those inherent in sharing existence freely and in seeking the truth.

It would seem that if subjective certainty is possible in spite of the uncertainties created by tolerance, then action must be possible, too. Do these arguments, then, effectively dispose of the suspicion, expressed by radical critics, that a policy of tolerance is tacitly conservative?

Tolerance and Action

To be tolerant, certainly, is not simply to tolerate everything. At the very least, it is to support the *principle* of tolerance, and that means to support a social order governed in accordance with that principle. Doing that may entail occasional limitations on tolerance. Thus a tolerant person cannot logically be tolerant of terrorism. By the same token a tolerant person cannot be tolerant of economic conditions that effectively exclude some groups from the realm of public discourse, thus rendering tolerance irrelevant. It may be said that the tolerance criticised in the *Critique of Pure Tolerance* is highly *im*pure—a tolerance not affirmed as a matter of principle and in consequence overwhelmed by unfavorable economic conditions.

It must be acknowledged, nonetheless, that an incongruity exists between tolerance and action. To be tolerant is to allow the continuation of debate, whereas to act is to close debate. The decision that precedes action is a withdrawal of attention and a termination of discourse; further talk is a means to some end other than truth. If others are heard and reasoned with in the midst of action, that is not because they are comrades in inquiry but because they can thus be used for the attainment of the ends that are sought. Inquiring discourse is supplanted by persuasion. For these reasons it cannot be denied that tolerance contains a bias toward inaction. Nor can it be denied that this bias has consequences in practice. These are often apparent in a capitalist society. The hesitancy inherent in tolerance is exploited by selfish interests. This is particularly manifest when an issue that could be rationally resolved—for example, the dangers of smoking—is kept artificially open and thus undecided.

Moreover, the actions of tolerant people are bound to be different in quality, if not in substance or purpose, from the actions of others. The difference comes from the margin of communality. Communal tolerance is incompatible, for example, with actions conceived as determinations of an absolutely reliable agent, like the Catholic church or the Communist party (in the eyes of some of their members), or as requirements of a complete and perfect plan. Communal tolerance is incompatible also with actions arising from the conception of some particular agent (the Catholic church, the Communist party) or system (capitalism, communism) as the source of all evil. Further, tolerance must encourage a realization that all action, however necessary, is an application of power and in that way evil. In sum, if tolerance is not unequivocally opposed to action, it does cast over action a shadow of irresolution and regret.

Is this not, however, all to the good? Some will feel that it is not. In America, not only on the Left but among conscientious people in general, there is a strong predisposition toward action. Anyone questioning the efficacy of action is apt to arouse impatience and even suspicion. The single and overriding imperative is that of "getting things done." This attitude probably reflects both the traditional pragmatism of Americans and alarm concerning the state of our world.

Yet the results of action in its most ambitious forms are almost invariably disappointing. The Russian Revolution gave rise to one of the worst tyrannies in the history of the world; British socialism has not prevented, and has perhaps helped to bring about, serious disorders in the industrial system; the American New Deal did not end the Depression, and successive waves of reform have left the nation with a burdensome and inequitable welfare system, inadequate housing, indefensible inequalities of wealth, and numerous other serious economic derangements. These comments do not imply conservatism. Human beings have to do what they can to eradicate injustices of the kind that come from unregulated capitalism. Action is not only a utilitarian but a moral necessity—in our times, an indispensable expression of the will to subordinate industrial power and wealth to the imperatives of community.

But the necessity of action is a tragic necessity. The exuberance normally manifest among those initiating great programs of change is singularly inappropriate.

So strong is modern man's faith in action that he persists in thinking that in spite of past failures we will eventually succeed in making society what we wish it to be. But the dangers and uncertainties of action are not merely accidental; as we noted earlier, they arise from an inalterable human characteristic—finitude. Man is not wholly transcendent. Partially immanent in nature and history, he cannot foresee all of the consequences of his actions. His very ontological situation imposes on all action a probability of disappointment.

And we must remember in this connection another point already mentioned: that action means power and power objectification. Others are to be used, circumvented, or ignored; they are to be heard and addressed only so far as the ends of action thus are served. To engage in action is at least provisionally to forget that each human being is an end, not merely a means, and the moral danger of action is that this will be permanently forgotten. What Lord Acton said of power can be said of action as well: "it tends to corrupt."

If action is a tragic necessity, then the attitudes neither of typical conservatives nor of typical radicals are altogether fitting. There is needed a nonconservative willingness to act along with a nonradical hesitancy and humility. These are incongruous qualities, but both together seem to be implicit in the margin of communality that is required by tolerance. To be concerned for that margin is to be concerned for community and thus to feel, in the midst of estrangement and injustice, the necessity of action; it is also to feel that every action must be followed by an interval of inaction, by an opportunity for the free response on which the fruitfulness of action depends. One might see in the margin of communality granted by tolerance a rule for transcending ideology and gaining political maturity, for learning civility.

Tolerance and Civility

I have suggested that the historical realization of community is not an appropriate object of action and is not probable. The objection might be made, however, that the same is true of a tolerant society: it cannot be produced by action, and if tolerance requires so delicate an inner balance as the preceding discussion implies, it cannot be expected that many people will be spontaneously tolerant. In what way, then, is tolerance a more feasible ideal than community? An answer might be found in a concept introduced in the opening chapter—the concept of civility.

Civility may be broadly defined as autonomous participation in history. "Autonomous" means both consciously chosen and irreducible to any set of socially defined responsibilities; "participation in history" means consciousness of and responsibility in relation to the problems of mankind generally. Some of the most impressive examples of civility are found among intellectuals who have been forced into alienated positions but have continued in solitude to inquire into public problems and, so far as possible and appropriate, to act in relation to them. Thucydides, Machiavelli, and Max Weber all illustrate the simultaneous independence and involvement that constitutes civility. Perhaps the supreme example of civility is Socrates, at once entirely autonomous and thoroughly communal.

Civility may be thought of as the inner fortress of community. In periods of disintegration and inhumanity the single individual may, through civility, sustain bonds of a kind with all human beings. Today, many feel historical despair; others remain fiercely determined to transform society. Civility is an effort to stand clear of both extremes, neither falling into political despondency nor counting on historical transformation.

I suggest that this civil balance, this solitary communality, is roughly the same as tolerance, provided tolerance is interpreted in a communal fashion. In the first place, to be tolerant is to be autonomous. Tolerance is an individualizing attitude. It disengages the one practicing it from every kind of fanaticism and institutional commitment. To admit that the ideas of someone who differs from me may be true is to admit that my own ideas may be false, and to acknowledge that there is room in the world for parties and groups to which I do not adhere is to relativize those to which I do adhere. In other words, to be genuinely tolerant is to be detached from all historical absolutes and in this way to be a distinct center of responsibility.

At the same time, however, to be tolerant is to recognize others as beings with whom discourse is possible. Thus the same act that establishes one as a separate and responsible being also establishes a civil relationship; one is linked with others through the possibility of speech. Not that recognizing this possibility fulfills one's responsibilities to mankind or constitutes the whole of civility. One must also be ready to act. But to act legitimately and wisely one must observe the margin of communality. Political action cannot possibly be rightly conceived and carried out without prior recognition that those in relation to whom one acts are beings with whom one *can* in some circumstances—and *should* when possible—speak. This recognition is the substance of communal tolerance.

The civil relationship is without any ultimate boundaries. It may be centered in a particular people or nation—all of the exemplars of civility cited above were in some sense patriots—but it cannot be thus confined. If it is unrestricted by historical absolutes, it is all-inclusive. Borrowing a phrase from Hegel, civility is "world-historical," a kind of global attentiveness and availability.

It should not be thought of as something very grandiose, however. One of the most vivid images of civility, as an effort to understand and be a part of history, is Tolstoy's picture of Pierre Bezukhov absurdly floundering about in the filth and blood of the Battle of Borodino. A civil person must be, like Pierre, ready for faith and human relationships, but inquiring and uncommitted; he is apt to be, in the pattern of Pierre, uncertain in his beliefs and hesitating in action; and he may be as ineffective and ludicrous as was Pierre. Such qualities are not widely admired in our time. But it could be that the decency of the future is as dependent on people like Pierre, capable of humane hesitation, as on heroes of action.

VI / PARADOXICAL PATRIOTISM

Patriotism today does not command much respect, particularly not among writers and intellectuals. It is the sovereign and rational individual, not the nation, that is admired. The individual, it is felt, should be more independent and critical than serious patriotism seems to allow: he should feel free to ignore, judge, or leave his native society. Admiring the free and rational individual, enlightened people are likely to regard the nation with an astringent and confident moral skepticism. The nation is seen as thirsty for power and morally insensitive, a constant threat both to liberty and to peace.

Certainly individuals deserve respect, even the limitless respect expressed in saying that the individual is an end and not a means; and certainly nations ought to be regarded suspiciously. One may nevertheless feel that the enlightened person's disdain for patriotism too casually and completely discounts the significance that a society has in the lives of its members. The individual is far more closely bound to his society than is generally acknowledged. For one thing, the individual is not as free and rational as he is often taken to be, and consequently his society is his fate. But he is not bound to society by necessity alone. He is related through his society to mankind and also to being itself, or transcendence. In this way he is bound to society by duty as well as by fate. Recognizing the bonds of fate and duty amounts to a kind of patriotism.

But recognizing these bonds does not imply that society is perfect or even very good; it does not imply any revision of the unfavorable view of society to which earlier reflections have led. Society is always more or less impersonal and coercive. Society is not community and does not unite its members in their essential being and in freedom.

Yet it is society, not community, to which a patriot is loyal. Hence the paradoxical character of patriotism. Societies, in their immensity and their prolonged existence, invite deification. But in view of their actual character, deification is a moral enormity. Hence patriotism has value only when it manifests a loyalty that is free of idolatry. Patriotism is fitting only when it arises from a lucid and perhaps reluctant "nevertheless."

We need not decide what sort of society—whether city, nation, or culture, for example—is qualified to be an object of loyalty. Perhaps only one general rule applies, and that is comprehensiveness. As Aristotle pointed out, society reaches full development only when it offers all that is essential for living well; a family or village would not be an appropriate object of patriotic attachment. But in some circumstances a city-state or a feudal domain might be. Today the most fitting object of loyalty for most people is a nation-state. But loyalty might in some circumstances appropriately be granted to a nation that has not become a state, to a people that has been conquered and dispersed by a foreign aggressor, or to a cultural area such as Europe. Within limits this is a matter of personal decision rather than objective definition. It would be difficult to say, for example (the issue of slavery aside), whether Robert E. Lee's decision to fight on the side of Virginia in 1861 was right or wrong.

Society and Fate

The common notion that an individual or a group can stand apart from society, carry on a completely distinctive life, and perhaps even become a source of renewal or revolution, is unrealistic. If it were valid, how could anthropologists, sociologists, and historians describe the various societies of the past and present? They would encounter a chaos defying scholarly study and generalization. Societies are describable only because individuals and groups within them conform more or less to common norms.

Moreover, the idea of individual or group independence is in conflict not only with facts but with almost any reasonable concept of human nature. Surely man is subject in some degree to causal determination, and many of the causes acting on him derive from society. But even if man is wholly a self-chosen being, as Sartre contends, he must choose from the restricted range of alternatives that society provides.

Not only are there many conceivable selves that he cannot choose because of circumstances set by society; there are innumerable selves compatible with the potentialities of human nature that, due to limits society puts on his mind, he cannot even imagine.

A person cannot sever himself from his native society by physically abandoning it. Society is a prime determinant of character, sensibility, and beliefs, and these remain in the structure of the expatriate self. Some of these characteristics he may expunge through arduous labor of self-transformation; but some will persist despite all efforts to remove them, and some will remain unidentified, constituting the ground, as it were, on which the person stands in asserting his independence. Hence revolutionary groups are likely to recreate many aspects of the society against which they are revolting, and the most creative individuals seem not so much to rise above their national characteristics as to reflect them with exceptional purity. Thus, as often noted, both the French revolutionaries of the eighteenth century and the Russian Bolsheviks established regimes in many ways like those they had overthrown. As for creative individuals, was not Socrates, in addition to being an incomparable individual, also thoroughly Athenian? D. H. Lawrence, exile and rebel, hated by many of his countrymen, once remarked that he was English "in the teeth" of England itself.

None of this is new. Awareness that the lives of individuals are confined and shaped by society has been commonplace since the beginnings of social and political philosophy in ancient Greece. This awareness has been dimmed by modern individualism, however, and at present various conceptions of individual and group independence are widely accepted. For example, many assume that a serene and orderly life can be carried on in the home, in spite of tension and disorder in the surrounding society. Others, especially in the universities, think of educational institutions as places apart from society, places where new ways of living can be imagined and inaugurated. Finally, Christians often take it for granted that lives of religious devotion can be carried on through the churches even though society at large is highly secular. Briefly to examine these three views may help to bring out the truth tacitly denied in each of them: that society severely limits the possibilities of uniqueness, that it does this not just through legal and moral prohibition but through inscribing itself so deeply in individuals that they represent society even when they are trying to reject it, and that society in this way is a fate.

The ascendancy of society in the home is manifest today in the inability of families to withstand the disintegration afflicting the industrialized nations. One of the most painful elements in modern life is alienation; individuals are deprived of substantial relationships with one another, with their places of birth, with nature, even with the past and future. In these circumstances the family, often idealized for its intimacy and warmth, cannot maintain its cohesion. It is divided by the fissures running through the rest of society. The forces that fragment towns and neighborhoods also break up the extended family; the inaccessibility of nature spells a closed and confining home; the strangeness of the past and the ominousness of the future occasion disagreements between generations. The emptiness of a commercialized culture leaves the family without symbols for dignifying and interpreting its life. The inanities of popular entertainment filter into intimate family relationships. And hostilities arising from frustrations in the surrounding society are often directed against members of one's immediate family. In short, it is almost impossible for the family to be a community without communal relations surrounding and supporting it.

Schools are larger and more imposing institutions than families. Are they any more independent of society? It is doubtful that they are, in spite of the hopes vested in them by idealists. To begin with, they are established by society to transmit its skills, knowledge, and values; they are established to be representative, not unique. Their status is determined not merely by financial dependence, however, but also by spiritual dependence. Teachers and administrators have not descended from above; they have been shaped by society. And the students are not simply raw materials to be processed and formed by educational engineers; they are subject to many formative powers other than those of the school. The whole society is the primary educator, or miseducator. "The public itself," as Plato said, "is the greatest of all sophists."[1]

As for the churches, here perhaps is the main source of the notion that a group can be different and apart from the surrounding society. In

1. Plato, *The Republic*, trans. Francis MacDonald Cornford (New York: Oxford University Press, 1945), 199.

the eyes of early Christians, society was no longer what it had been for the Greeks, a realm in which all human potentialities could come to realization. Rather, it was a setting within which a distinct and superior association, the Church, could minister to man's highest potentialities. But the independence of the Church did not depend on its higher purposes; it derived from grace. It could easily be assumed that the influence of society on the Church was negligible, for the latter was under higher determinants. This faith has perhaps never been more heavily relied upon than during the past two or three centuries, with the rise of secularism. Christians have been able to assure themselves that religious life could be vigorously carried on within the churches, unaffected by society. Is it not clear, however, that this has not happened? It was clear to critics as deeply opposed in other ways as Kierkegaard and Marx. Both saw in the churches less of the faith of authentic Christians than of the interests and attitudes of the bourgeoisie. And looking back in history, it should not be forgotten that although in one sense the Church converted the Empire, in another sense the Empire converted the Church. With its law, hierarchy, and centralized authority, the Church came to be formed on an imperial model. This happened in spite of the immense creative forces working through it and in spite of a faith fundamentally hostile to law, hierarchy, and centralized authority.

But is man's involvement in society merely a matter of necessity and not also of obligation? Socrates, discussing with friends their proposal that he escape from prison and thus avoid execution, imagines that "the laws" say to him, "Since you were brought into the world and nurtured and educated by us, can you deny . . . that you are our child and slave, as your fathers were before you?"[2] Socrates acceded to this suggestion and, as the child and slave of the laws, gave up his life. Being an Athenian, he discovered, was not only a fate but also a duty.

Society and Love

What is the scope of love? On the one hand, it may seem that we can love only those whom we intimately know. If that were so, society would be merely utilitarian, a device for serving needs and not a set of relationships with any value in themselves. On the other hand, perhaps

2. Plato, *Crito*, in *The Dialogues of Plato*, trans. Benjamin Jowett (2 vols.; New York: Random House, 1920), I, 434–435.

love is not so exclusively personal as it seems. Perhaps it draws one toward all humanity and perhaps it binds one to society by something more than calculations of expediency. In asking about the scope of love we thus confront two plausible answers.

The moral intuition of Western man is decisively on the side of the second answer. Both the Hebrews and the Greeks of ancient times began with narrow loyalties but neither remained within the limits of those loyalties. The tribalism of the Hebrews developed into the universalism of Isaiah, who prophesied that God would "gather all nations and tongues" to see his glory.[3] The mission of Jesus, apparently thought of at some moments by Jesus Himself as a mission to the Hebrews alone, was construed by Paul as the axis of all earthly history, offering salvation not only to all men—"for there is no difference between the Jew and the Greek"—but to "the whole creation," which "groaneth and travaileth in pain together until now."[4] And finally, from the parochialism of the Greek *polis* arose the Stoic vision of a city including all mankind. Such universalism has, of course, been occasionally challenged. Writing in a period of historical confusion and despair, Epicurus advised men to ignore the encompassing society and concentrate on relations with friends; in another discouraging time, two thousand years later, Thomas Hobbes argued that society means nothing to us except protection. Views of this kind have gained some assent. It is appealing in times of unusual strain in the surrounding world to think that one's life may legitimately be devoted to private friendship or to self-preservation. But Western man has never been won away from the faith of Isaiah, Paul, and the Stoics that the force binding him to a few also binds him in some way to all.

But does it bind him to *society*? No society includes more than a portion of mankind. Why should anyone think that a bond with all humanity entails allegiance to Athens, or England, or the United States—to an association which, although wider than any circle of personal relationships, is much narrower than the range of love? And there is another difficulty. If society is essentially impersonal and hierarchical, then it divides its members not only from people in other societies but also from one another. Love, it may seem, calls for communal, not

3. Isaiah 66:18
4. Romans 10:12 and 8:22 respectively.

social relationships. Briefly, neither in scope nor in character does society answer to the requirements of love.

Reflecting on the fact that no single society includes all of mankind, it may be noted first that it is not wholly unreasonable to look upon society as a surrogate for mankind. As pointed out at the beginning of this essay, the one rule for identifying a social unit deserving loyalty is comprehensiveness. It must be inclusive enough to provide all that is needed for living well. Defined in this way, a society such as a city-state or a nation-state has a kind of universality. It provides what is conceived by the rulers of the society, and necessarily by most members as well, as all of the opportunities necessary for man to live as man. It provides what is conceived to be an appropriate sphere of life, not just for a certain number of human beings but for humanity. And while such universality is never attained in fact, it is occasionally approximated and the conception of it is essential in any claim to independence or sovereignty.

Moreover, while a particular society is of lesser scope than mankind, it is of greater reality. It constitutes an explicit and operative structure of rights and duties—not just in the constitution or even in the legal order as a whole, but in the entire, intricate order of its life. It is, in this sense, a reality in the world. Mankind, however, is not. It is a mere numerical totality—an abstraction. It is also, of course, an ideal of human brotherhood and universal peace. As an ideal, it is of great importance, but it is not an actual sphere of life. To be a citizen of the world is not more, but far less, than to be a citizen of Great Britain or France.

Still, should not any society to which one is loyal include all human beings? Can one realize his full humanity through loyalty to any association of lesser extent than the entire human race? These questions deserve careful thought. Affirmative answers would condemn existing societies and imply that love must look beyond them. Negative answers, however, would sanction large but limited societies, such as the nation-states of the present day, and would warn us against trying to draw any nearer to universality in our organized life. It would open the way to a paradoxical patriotism. It is the negative answer, I suggest, that is true.

The reason it is true is indicated in the story of the Tower of Babel, where the origin of diversity among earthly societies is mythically described: every society is a kingdom of pride and should be limited in its geographical extent in order to encourage it to limit its pretensions. To enclose all mankind in one society would make it easier than it is at present to think that one particular human type is identical with man in his universal essence; and it would make it easier for the rulers of the one global society to mistake themselves for gods. Further, every possible escape would be foreclosed. If all the world were America, being an American would be far more trying than it is; if all the world were dictatorial Russia, being Russian might be unbearable. The plurality of societies reminds us that every society is drastically imperfect; and establishing possibilities of exile and emigration helps us to realize that the destiny of an individual is not equivalent to his role in a particular society.

This suggests a reversal of the principles underlying traditional patriotism. It is never the case that a social order ought to be limited in scope because it is absolutely good as it is, or even superior to all others, and might be weakened through being widened or contaminated through inclusion of foreign peoples. On the contrary, every social order should be limited in scope because it is *not* absolutely good or decidedly superior. It follows that one ought to inhabit one's society with humility rather than pride, and with a consciousness of being part of the whole human race in its various social forms, none to be deified and none to be thoughtlessly looked down upon or condemned. A society of limited scope may, in this way, link one with mankind. Must it not divide one, however, from those within?

The very nature of society implies that it must. As we have seen, society means function, rank, expediential calculation. Society is not merely indifferent to untrammeled and imaginative communication, but ordinarily fears it—and sometimes with good reason. The Crucifixion symbolizes the antithesis between society and love. Does it follow, however, that an individual should have no more to do with society than is dictated by expediency or force? Is love irrelevant? The mere fact that society is needed, and that without its anticommunal activities community would be impossible, shows that no such simple inferences can be drawn.

Society is necessary for meeting basic physical needs; it is necessary for assuring the order without which there are few opportunities for speaking and listening; it is necessary for developing and maintaining the cultural sophistication on which communication depends. These functions are unlikely to be effectively fulfilled without help from the kind of people who are practised in communication but not much at home in society at large. This implies that it is apt to be those who spontaneously care least about society who owe it their support and that the basis of this obligation is that which estranges them from society—their devotion to community. Man as a communal being does not draw nearer to community through disengagement from society, but compromises his very adherence to the principle of community.

Moreover, he does not merely compromise a principle; he impairs actual relationships. Epicurus advocated withdrawal from society and concentration on personal friendship. But this is to speak as though society were merely a casual habitation. If it is a fate, if it enters into the innermost being of its members, then a relationship between persons who set themselves apart from society and try to find true selfhood in that which is unaffected by society is a relationship between abstractions; or rather, since abstractions of that sort are impossible, it is a relationship between illusions.

Entering into community is not a way of departing from society, but rather of transmuting society by bringing it into the sphere of critical intelligence and interpersonal space. Communication that excluded the affairs of society at large would be trivial, and a personal relationship confined to matters of concern only to those involved would necessarily be impoverished. The best personal relationship that can be imagined might be numerically exclusive, but in the scope of its inquiring concern it would be universal.

Fate is overcome by being lived through and shared. Man in his communality must struggle with society without repudiating it. He must be a determinate person, identifiable in terms of his place within a particular society. His humanity lies in his being the one he is fated to be and in doing this in a lucid and inquiring fashion—in a communal fashion. Man must struggle with society in order to turn the circumstances of his life into media of interpersonal relations, and thus from fate into truth.

But human beings do not seek relationships only with other human beings but also with transcendence—with ultimate being, conceived of as the source and goal of existence. It is possible to think that there is no such being. But man is profoundly interested in the question of whether there is, and he is in no position to give a demonstrable or dogmatic answer. It is thus appropriate for him to adopt an attitude of openness, a transcendental attentiveness. Such an attitude is rare and difficult. It requires of skeptics a sincere accessibility to something they consider highly unlikely—revelation; it requires of believers acknowledgment that God is not a being known and possessed. While openness toward transcendence is rare and difficult, however, it entirely befits our finitude. What I wish to suggest is that it depends on a participatory relationship with society.

Society and Transcendence

Summarily, openness toward transcendence depends on living lucidly in one's worldly situation and on sustaining a responsible relationship with other human beings. These things are done, according to preceding reflections, only through membership in society.

It is onerous to live within society. It is not merely to be in the company of many others; it is also to be subject to a host of risks and constraints. It is to be subject to the diseases, the economic scarcities, the wartime disasters, and the spiritual trials that affect whole societies. But looking at things from a broadly Hebraic and Christian standpoint, these conditions are not unrelated to man's interest in transcendence. Transcendence is discovered within the human situation, in the midst of fear and suffering. It is not reserved for a few who have escaped from the common hazards of existence into a state of secure and leisured contemplation. It is redemptive because it is accessible to man in his struggle with the burdens and terrors of fate.

Withdrawal from society is not only an evasion of fate, however, but also of other human beings. Someone who has abandoned his native country and has not permanently adopted another may, of course, spend a great deal of time with people. But such a person eschews all of the constraints inherent in having a settled place within a particular country. He is bound to no particular residence, vocation, or political order. In that way he holds aloof from the limits and hazards of the human state and is an alien in relation to mankind. Such alienation is not only social, however. It is also religious, if we follow the ancient idea expressed in Judaism, in ancient Greek philosophy, and in Christianity, that the love of God and the love of man are inseparable. "He that loveth not his brother whom he hath seen," asks John, "how can he love God whom he hath not seen?"[5] In our own terms: how can one who is not fully present with and open toward other human beings be open toward transcendence?

Dostoevsky believed that a person who has no country can have no God either. This can easily be dismissed as both socially and religiously reactionary. But to do so might, as the preceding comments indicate, be to miss an important truth. Following the Jewish and Christian traditions, there is a correspondence between transcendence and ordinary humanity. Someone who wishes genuinely to listen for the voice of transcendence (and this might be someone who doubts that there is any such voice to be heard) must therefore be willing to live and listen as an ordinary human being. That means being confined within a particular society, for that is the fate of almost everyone on earth.

Granting even this limited degree of religious significance to secular society is apt to go against the grain of people influenced by Christian traditions. To most Christians, society at large has seemed far too inclusive and miscellaneous an assemblage to have a place in any dialogue between transcendence and humanity. Thus Paul enjoins Christians against being "unequally yoked together with unbelievers." "What communion," he asks, "hath light with darkness?" And expressing the self-assurance that helped bring the Christian church into existence and the disdain for ordinary society that has long animated the members of the church, he concludes, "Wherefore come out from among them, and be ye separate."[6]

This is very much the contrary of the view I have just been urging. But is so severe a depreciation of ordinary society really Christian? Does it accord with the essentials of the faith that Paul himself expressed with such matchless power? The Christian God descends into the lives of common and sinful human beings. He speaks to people in lowly and even in disreputable occupations. It is true that some have seemed to be resolutely and hopelessly evil, and the biblical God is sometimes angry and punitive. Yet the biblical God is not only wrathful but also merciful and, according to the New Testament, "will have all men to be saved."[7]

5. I John 4:20
6. II Corinthians 6:14–17

7. I Timothy 2:4

The idea of predestination has been defended as a terrible and impenetrable divine mystery. But is not the thought of universal salvation also awesome?

Thus the very notion that there exists a distinction of eternal significance between the good and the evil, the elect and the damned, is perilous and questionable. How much more so, then, is the distinction so prejudicial to mundane society, including as it does all human beings and all occupations and activities, between the secular order and the church. It is no doubt appropriate for Christians to believe that the churches have a responsibility that rests on no other group. It is another matter, however, for them to assume that the churches monopolize or in any way command man's access to transcendence. Looked at realistically, it is certain that the churches are worldly, corruptible institutions. Looked at from the standpoint of faith, one may think that God so humbles his hearers that rather than claiming preeminence they should assume the posture of Job, who declared, when addressed by God out of the whirlwind, "Behold I am vile . . . I will lay my hand upon my mouth."[8] How could a church following that counsel look down contemptuously on society?

Thus disdain for society, the disdain that speaks in the injunction "Be ye separate," is not clearly required by Christian faith, despite all of the tendencies in that faith toward the depreciation of society. The Crucifixion symbolizes the antithesis of society and truth, society and love; but it also symbolizes the descent of God into society. Even the typical Christian assurance in the perfection and finality of God's self-disclosure in Christ need not be decisive. If Christianity embodies all truth, then instead of concluding that the truth is to be found nowhere else a Christian might logically conclude that Christianity is to be found, at least in fragments, everywhere. Christ may be foolishness to the Greeks, but the insights of the Greeks need not be foolishness to Christians.

"Except a corn of wheat fall into the ground and die," wrote John, "it abideth alone: but if it die, it bringeth forth much fruit."[9] We may think of society as the ground into which man must fall and of community—first of all with transcendence—as the fruit. We have no

8. Job 40:4
9. John 12:24

assurance of gaining such fruit. Our demonstrable knowledge leaves ample room for doubting its very possibility. My argument is only that in our finitude this is a matter we are incapable of rationally deciding. That is why it is incumbent on us to be open toward transcendence and in our openness to enter freely into those relationships that we encounter first as fate.

Paradoxical Patriotism

Summarizing, although society is in many ways antithetical to community, man as a communal being must participate in society. Otherwise, he lays claim to an elevation over circumstances that is not human. In doing that he alienates himself from other human beings, and this precludes community; it also precludes any possible relationship with transcendence.

This suggests that man should be related to society through a paradoxical loyalty—a loyalty not determined by the conviction that one's own society is very good or even superior to other societies, but by acquiescence in man's common fate. Natural affection of course should play a role. Our emotions bind us to the land where we have been born and have spent our lives. But emotions are ordinarily ambiguous, sometimes setting us against, as well as on the side of, our native society; and in any case, emotions do not constitute moral obligations. Our reflections here indicate that the obligations binding man to society are discovered in the realization that the relationships we seek, with human beings and with transcendence, depend on our being lucidly and responsibly human, and not more than human, and that being human means living within society. The exclamation, "My country, right or wrong!" usually is quoted to illustrate and condemn the amorality of patriotism. But if that exclamation were uttered by someone neither blind nor indifferent to moral distinctions, it might express a patriotism of another kind—a patriotism neither ignoring nor determined by the moral criticisms to which every nation is subject.

As a matter of theory, this patriotism is not easily explained. Yet it is certain that it exists. Human beings have often been bound to their native societies by a strange kind of love, a love not defeated by the moral failings of those societies, yet not amoral—hence a love at times expressed in protest, rebellion, exile, or martyrdom. Socrates stayed in

Athens, trying as "gadfly" to sting his city into moral consciousness and inquiry, although this very role depended on his awareness of Athenian degradation; and his refusal to escape from prison, and thus from death, came from his loyalty to the laws and institutions under which he had been unjustly condemned. In modern times, Dietrich Bonhoeffer evinced a loyalty to Germany more paradoxical than the loyalty of Socrates to Athens, for Bonhoeffer was loyal to a country governed by Hitler and the Nazis, a regime he hoped to see defeated in the war it had precipitated. Although he was in America after the outbreak of the war and could have stayed in America, Bonhoeffer felt obliged to return to Germany—in order to "share the trials of this time with my people" [10]—where he was executed for taking part in the Resistance.

No doubt patriotism has encouraged unintelligent and repressive attitudes. But this does not imply that patriotism in essence is unintelligent and repressive. Paradoxical patriotism has quite a different character from traditional patriotism.

1. Paradoxical patriotism arises from humility rather than the pride so common among patriots. That is what makes it paradoxical; it is a loyalty affirmed in spite of manifest imperfections. I do not adhere to my country because it is, to use the words of a well-known exponent of the patriotism of pride, "the Divine Idea as it exists on earth," [11] but because I am nothing more than a human being and do not want to exempt myself from the general conditions of human existence.

2. Humility prompts quite a different attitude toward fellow citizens than the attitude cultivated in traditional patriotism—a consciousness of their imperfections, along with a disinclination to condemn them. Fellow citizens are not primarily comrades in national glory but sharers in a collective life that is bound to be more or less base. They are bound to be sometimes unwise and cruel, particularly in their political attitudes and actions. But paradoxical patriotism entails subdued expectations, and it is possible only for those who accord fellow citizens that which they occasionally need themselves—a merciful suspension of judgment.

10. See Mary Bosanquet, *The Life and Death of Dietrich Bonhoeffer* (New York: Harper & Row, 1968).

11. Georg Wilhelm Friedrich Hegel, *The Philosophy of History*, trans. J. Sibree (Rev. ed.; New York: Willey Book Co., no date), 39.

3. Toward other societies a patriotism of humility implies openness rather than belligerence and merciful understanding rather than haughty superiority. Where loyalty is paradoxical, it constitutes a link with mankind rather than the usual patriotic illusion of exaltation above mankind. The existence of a world outside reminds one whose patriotism is paradoxical—and thus humble—of his country's imperfections; hence he looks outward in hope of communication, not of conquest.

Of course patriotism involves more than a grim willingness to share the human fate; there must, for example, be some degree of affection for one's people and respect for prevailing institutions. But these cannot be morally decisive. The governing principle of patriotism, in the complete absence of which it must turn into something uncivil and barbaric, is the will to share the conditions inherent in being human. Society is the place where one lives as a member of the human race by experiencing to the full man's finitude and plurality. If entering into society is to be put in terms of spatial movement, one must think of descent; and this metaphor brings to mind Plato's most powerful myth: society can be likened to the cave into which the philosopher must descend. By entering into that cave, man is not exalted but only joins the human race.

What Plato leaves out, however, in his conception of the philosopher's voluntary descent into the cave, is fate. This is left out, also, of another well-known doctrine concerning man's relationship with society, that of the social contract. Both Plato and the social contract theorists assumed that man could gain a position of complete transcendence over society and there decide in full rationality and freedom what his relationship with society should be. But man is born within the cave and can never completely and securely escape from it; continuing Plato's metaphor—although taking issue with his argument—one's eyes never become fully adjusted to the sunlight. Patriotism thus is paradoxical not only in being a loyalty that overlooks imperfections but also in being an act of freedom that acquiesces in necessity.

This is not to deny every right of dissociation or resistance, however. A patriotism that is paradoxical in its grounds must be paradoxical also in its expressions. This brings us to a question that has repeatedly called out for consideration in the course of this discussion but has so far been ignored: what does participation in society mean?

Cooperation and Resistance

It is easy to specify certain elementary forms of participation in society. (1) A person becomes a member of society by linking his natural life with it, and this is done in two primary ways: by residing within its boundaries and by establishing a family there. The latter is a particularly imperious commitment. One cannot sever relations with a family nearly so readily as with a territory alone, and these relations usually bind him in other ways as well—to job, to home, and so forth. (2) One participates in society by acceding to its official demands—by obeying the laws, paying taxes, and fulfilling military duties. (3) Participation may consist partly in carrying on an occupation that society regards as useful. One does not merely live within the society and meet its legal demands, but also fulfills an approved function. (4) Finally, participation would be incomplete without accepting some form of political responsibility, for politics is the activity through which society considers and shapes its life. For Aristotle, looking upon man as a "political animal" and social membership as preeminently political activity, the primary requirement was that of holding office. However, it perhaps suffices, and for most people in a mass democracy it must suffice, to support in some way others who hold office or seek office.

In all of these ways, one participates by fitting in. But the antagonism of society and community implies that fitting in does not adequately define the responsibilities of one who joins society for the sake of community. Wholly acquiescing in the established order would at times involve a betrayal of community. Today in America those who manufacture and advertise cigarettes are fulfilling the duties of an occupation that is still reputable. According to Hannah Arendt, even Adolf Eichmann, organizing and supervising the deportations of European Jews to Hitler's death camps, performed his work in the spirit of a loyal and efficient servant of the state, merely meeting the duties of his office.[12] Unqualified cooperation with an established society clearly entails violation of communal bonds, the degree to which it does this depending on the character of the society. If the imperative of *social* participation derives from the higher imperative of *communal* participation,

12. Hannah Arendt, *Eichmann in Jerusalem: A Report on the Banality of Evil* (Rev. ed.; New York: Viking Press, 1963).

and if society and community are not wholly congruent, then participation in society requires something more complicated than filling a certain place within the existing order.

Thus we are brought to the concept of resistance as another potential form of participation. Anything from a slight and unostentatious withholding of cooperation to armed revolution may be classified as resistance; anything within this range may aim at rectifying injustice and bettering society and may in this way be participatory. Blacks who boycott a bus line or a store to bring about racial integration are not merely opposing society; through resistance, they are participating in society.

Every form of cooperative participation has a corresponding form of resistant participation. (1) Residence within the territory of a society is not an unchallengeable natural decree, like one's physical structure. While expatriation is ordinarily very difficult, and nothing can dispel the fate inherent in being born in a particular time and place, even the remote possibility of expatriation enhances the possibilities of basing fate on freedom. Leaving one's native land can in some circumstances be an effective form of participation, and a lifelong expatriate like Pablo Casals may live as a patriot. (2) Laws may be disobeyed, taxes and military service withheld. Civil disobedience is ordinarily far more troublesome than obedience and is a more certain sign than obedience that the duties of participation are taken seriously. When disobedience is public and the penalties attached to it are accepted without protest, its participatory character is particularly emphasized. (3) Rather than merely carrying on an occupation, one may follow a vocation. While a mere occupation is entered upon in response to social opportunities and necessities, a vocation is pursued in response to the demands of the self and, perhaps, of transcendence. To pursue a vocation is to take part in society, but not necessarily in a way that meets the approval of society; men are often honored for their occupations but execrated for their vocations. (4) Instead of following the rules of the political system, one may engage in political activity that is unsanctioned by the system or even threatening to the system. Political resistance should never be undertaken lightly, but its possible legitimacy is incontestable. A constitutional order deserves deep respect, but its value is still only conditional; community is of higher value.

In sum, the communal stance—the attitude of one disposed for communication but cognizant of the just claims of society—is both cooperative and resistant. This duality is ineradicable, tracing back to the duality of society and community.

The result is that the posture of communal man cannot be assured and relaxed. There is no rule prescribing exactly the proper balance between cooperation and resistance. This balance depends on infinitely variable circumstances, and it is determined both by demands of conscience and by calculations of expediency. It requires a spiritual and political poise in which one is never subservient yet is continually responsible. The example of Socrates again is pertinent. Socrates persisted in his communal work of carrying on moral inquiry among the youth and leaders of Athens in defiance of the most emphatic wishes and prejudices of his society. Yet having finally, in his fidelity to community, been subjected to baseless accusations and to an unjust sentence of death, he refused to save his life by escaping from prison because that would have been contrary to the law. So paradoxical a combination of resistance and cooperation is irreducible to any single moral rule. It can be expressed only in the form of a living—and thoroughly communal —personality.

The posture of communal man is likely to be difficult also, as the example of Socrates suggests, because it is likely to entail estrangement. Authentic communality may ironically force one into isolation. Who is more communal—a businessman who does everything that society expects and is rarely alone, or a gifted but uncompromising and solitary artist?

The paradoxes of a truly communal patriotism may be incomprehensible to witnesses. Hence communal man may be deprived of recognition. He may be deprived of recognition, moreover, not only in his own time but in all times. Here the example of Socrates can be misleading, for Socrates, while suffering dishonor during his life, has been honored ever since. The average person can expect nothing of the kind and must consequently be prepared, as the price of communality, for oblivion. Most of us, after all, are simply not distinguished enough to claim a place in the memory of future ages. But even those who are have no assurance that such a claim will be granted. If society cannot be relied on to recognize and respect communal fidelity when it first appears, why assume that it will unfailingly do so later on? Posterity is merely society after it has had time to reconsider. Although some who at first are ignored later are recognized, to suppose that this process is infallible is a kind of social idolatry. Perhaps all of this is of little concern to most people; but it does bear on the character of paradoxical patriotism. The point is that such patriotism has little to do with the quest for renown and "immortal glory" that figures so prominently among exemplars of the patriotism of pride. A patriotism expressed in resistance is altogether suitable only to those not intimidated by the prospect of powerlessness and lasting oblivion. In the nature of the case, no names can be mentioned as examples; only general categories are known to us. Among the latter, however, we might recall Bonhoeffer's many fellow countrymen who opposed Hitler and in consequence died in Nazi prisons, totally without public notice at the time and little remembered since.

Conclusion

The political outlook we have reached is a variation on Aristotle. Man is seen as a social and political being, but society and the state are viewed pessimistically. In Aristotle, there is no distinction between society and community; the *polis*, as fully developed society, is identical with community. Hence man realizes his nature fully through participation in the *polis*, and patriotism—which can easily be read into Aristotle's doctrine—is nonparadoxical. But if society and community are not altogether congruous and man is a communal being, then membership in society cannot be directly and unambiguously fulfilling. At best, it is the way man accepts the burden of his impaired humanity and opens himself to the renascent humanity found in community. But the realization of that humanity cannot be the natural unfoldment within a favorable social environment that Aristotle envisioned. Between society and selfhood there must intervene the "nevertheless" of a paradoxical loyalty. Before bearing fruit, the seed must "fall into the ground and die."

VII / COMMUNICATION, ACTION, AND HISTORY

We tend today to view history according to one or the other of two extreme interpretations. On one side, history is insignificant, something the individual would do well to ignore. On the other side, it is not only supremely significant, being an order of events in which each one can discern his own destiny; it is rationally comprehensible, and perhaps even controllable. Kierkegaard exemplifies the former interpretation, Marx the latter. For Kierkegaard, reacting against Hegel's grandiose historical speculations, history was mainly a distraction. This was true even of the history of Christianity, for it was a Christian's task to thrust aside the intervening centuries and become contemporary with Christ. Marx, on the other hand, reaffirmed Hegel's conviction that history must and can be comprehended. Marx believed that through history humanity attains its full stature, and the individual thus sees in history the development of his own essential being. The historical record, moreover, is potentially a matter of perfect rational understanding; the past is an object of scientific inquiry. The point is not, as in Hegel, however, just to understand what has happened. Marx's view of history is imbued with the same activism that is expressed in his famous comment on efforts to interpret the world: "the point . . . is to change it." [1]

In view of ideas developed in the course of these reflections, however, both of these interpretations must be questioned. If we are communal beings, we cannot legitimately turn away from history; here

1. "Theses on Feuerbach," XI, in Karl Marx, *On Religion* (New York: McGraw-Hill, 1974), Vol. V of *The Karl Marx Library*, ed. and trans. Saul K. Padover.

Kierkegaard is much further from the truth than is Marx. But on the other hand, if we are finite and imperfect, we cannot rationally know history or deliberately control it. We are deeply concerned with history, but in no sense are we its possessors. Preceding reflections suggest that the clue to man's proper relationship with history may be found in the concept of communication. In studying and reflecting on history man seeks, above all else, to overcome mankind's tragic dispersal in time; and he does this by acts more akin to communication than to objective investigation. Historiography and the philosophy of history are communal undertakings, carried on in resistance to the alienating power of time. Our historical knowledge is in the nature of an all-inclusive, albeit drastically imperfect, community. These, at any rate, are the hypotheses with which we shall begin.

The first question facing us is posed by Kierkegaard: why should we care about history at all? Is not burying the dead a task for the dead?

The Individual and History

Magnifying the importance of history, it has often been charged, is disrespectful of individual human beings. The compass of history is so vast and the perspectives so distant that individuals become imperceptible and unimportant. Thus in the stupendous dramas depicted by thinkers such as Augustine and Hegel, the single person is almost nothing. *The City of God* and *The Philosophy of History* are cruel works in their preoccupation with the "world-historical" and in their apparent indifference to the individual lives ruined in the accomplishment of world-historical purposes. Nicolas Berdyaev attacked the doctrine of progress on the grounds that it sanctions sacrificing earlier to later generations, and in this way he drew attention to the apparent antagonism between the individual and history. "History takes no notice of personality," he wrote, "of its individual unrepeatability, its uniqueness and irreplaceability. . . . Every average man is turned into a means to serve the interests of average humanity."[2]

One is tempted to draw the simple and appealing conclusion that we should forget the remote past and the distant future and concentrate on those persons with whom we share the present moment. Why should

2. Nicolas Berdyaev, *Slavery and Freedom*, trans. R. M. French (New York: Charles Scribner's Sons, 1944), 255.

we not? Is it not a kind of betrayal of the living to become preoccupied with generations that are dead or not yet born? The strange truth, I suggest, is the very opposite: that we betray the living by *forgetting* the dead and unborn.

To begin with, every human relationship, even the most intimate and personal, is historical and can be fully realized only by realizing its historical dimensions. Not only is the situation in which it arises historical; the personality, character, and beliefs of the participants are also historical. The person in my immediate presence embodies a generation, and a generation embodies history. Nor is it only the recent past or the near future to which the mystery of the person before us invites our attention. We could fully understand one person and fully participate in a present relationship only if we understood man's ultimate origins and most distant possibilities—the beginning and the end of history.

But we are not concerned only with those whom we personally know or only with the living. It is not in spite of the dead that we study and reflect upon history, but because of them. In justifying the study of history, we are apt to be self-consciously hardheaded; we try to show that a knowledge of history brings practical advantages. I suggest, however, that such "realism" deludes us and that it is not utilitarian calculation that turns us toward history as much as it is the sense that we cannot, as human beings who now live, ignore the multitudes of human beings who have already lived and have died. Our aim is not even so practical as getting to know human nature. Nor is it so abstract. We wish simply to get in touch with concrete human beings whom we are dimly aware of in the darkness of the past. The passage of time separates us, generation from generation, the living from the dead. We struggle against our alienation when we inquire into the past and try to make it present. History in its harsh actuality divides us; history as story and philosophy partially heals. Man is concerned with all mankind, and his concern with history is a sign of this universality.

Even someone concentrating wholly upon the living, however, would find history demanding his attention. One cannot enter into a serious relationship without being conscious that it is temporary. It is bound to disintegrate, if not simply through the ephemerality of most human bonds then through death. Here we may think first of intimate personal relationships; but larger relationships, with a place or a nation, also are temporary. Time—and thus history—is the mortal enemy of every community. It is likely that a concern with history often originates as an effort to dissolve this enmity—to discover how history can be halted or to see whether in its ultimate ends it may not be an ally rather than an enemy. Thus for Plato, the rule of philosophers was a way not only of uniting men but also, at least for awhile, of stopping history; Augustine sought to show that the fall of Rome was only an episode in the enactment of God's irresistible intent to end time and establish the City of God; and Hegel and Marx interpreted historical conflicts as expressions of a force that would at last bring authentic and enduring community. Man finds it intolerable that his life should be altogether subordinated to time. And trying to dwell within the present moment and to ignore its ephemerality provides no escape from this situation. If we try to concentrate on present relationships, we find history robbing us of these relationships, and that compels us to ask whether the loss is unavoidable and final—to study and reflect on history.

Perhaps *love* is not too strong a word to summarize these concerns. We are drawn to history because it presents us with the few whom we love; we are drawn to history also because it includes and can be made partially to disclose the multitudes of the dead whom we also in some sense love; and we reflect upon history because the passage of time mocks our love both for a few and for all mankind. For all of these reasons we investigate and speculate upon the past and the future. To suggest that love is our primary motive is not to deny practical motives as well: historical study no doubt acquaints us with human nature, for example, and it helps to reduce our hopes to realistic proportions. But if historical scholarship, reflection, and teaching all had to be justified purely for their practical value, we would probably classify them among our useful but dispensable activities. And if these activities were proven to be entirely destitute of practical value, we would find ourselves still devoted to them.

A final bond with history must be noted. It is tempting, for the sake of symmetry, to call this bond "the love of God," but that would be too simple. It would be more accurate to speak of man's *interest* in God—an interest that may take the form of love, of disbelief and hostility, or merely of concern for the grounds of meaning and value. Corresponding with these forms, man's interest in God has three main sources: hunger for a plenitude of being that is seemingly available only in and through the divine; the conviction that religious reverence is incompatible with man's full dignity and freedom; and finally the belief, in itself without either love or hostility, that God is our only security for certain values, such as the authority of ethical norms. Thus historical study and reflection may be prompted by a desire either to find traces of God in the world (Augustine, Hegel) or to show that the universe belongs solely to man (Comte, Marx).

From this standpoint, the central issue is that of meaning—whether history has meaning, and if it does, of what kind. If it could be shown that history is senseless, then it would be difficult to believe in God. Thus historical disasters call forth philosophical speculation on history. Augustine's philosophy of history was a response to the collapse of Rome and was an effort to reconcile this event with the Christian faith in an omnipotent and merciful God. On the other hand, religious faith can be shaken not only by showing that history is senseless but also by showing that it has a sense unrelated to the providence of God. An assault on faith was implicit in Marx's interpretation of history as made, deliberately or not, altogether by man.

To indicate summarily the breadth of concern—with humanity and with God—that draws us toward history, it might be said simply that man is a universal being. He is not indifferent to any aspect of those he loves or to any human beings who ever have lived or ever will live; he cannot ignore, even temporarily, the question of God. His universality can take the form of a will to power, but in essence it is something more basic—a will to relatedness or unity. It pits him against time, because time separates and destroys. And it definitively rules out the historical detachment that Kierkegaard advocated.

What we are considering is man's very being. Relationships are not added on to a person; they enter into one's very essence. A particular individual can be identified, therefore, only by family, profession, country, and so forth—in terms of how and with whom he has connections. To attribute universality to man is to assert that there is no natural limit to the scope of his being. He is not, for example, merely a "*polis* being," as Aristotle held. The universalism of politics and political thought in the Hellenistic Age shows this. Everything real has a claim on man's attention, but this claim is not from the outside; it is a claim of his own being.

This implies that man potentially, and in some measure actually, is microhistorical. Whereas from one point of view the person is within history, from another point of view history is within the person. What one searches for in history is not the distant and exotic but one's own full selfhood.

Here it seems to me that it is Hegel who was right, not Kierkegaard, even though Kierkegaard castigated Hegel for ignoring the concrete, living individual. There was no doubt a certain insensitivity to individuals in Hegel's thought; hence the cruelty of *The Philosophy of History*. The fact remains that Kierkegaard was insensitive to realities that Hegel understood. The individual in Kierkegaard's thought was a radical abstraction, not concrete man shaped by his times and concerned, in his universality, with all mankind. Redemption for Kierkegaard was re-demption *from* history, and that, for all of Kierkegaard's battles in behalf of "the existing individual," could not be redemption of the full, living human being.

While history is of compelling interest, however, it seems vast and incomprehensible. The dead and unborn are numberless and im-measurably distant. The train of events manifests little meaning, par-ticularly in so confusing and unhappy a time as ours. If it is true that we must concern ourselves with history, then we must ask how we can do so without cultivating illusions. Here too the concept of community may help.

Communication and History

History *is* beyond human comprehension; that is not merely an impres-sion. Owing probably to the success of science and technology, many people think of our relations with reality primarily in terms of exact knowledge and effective action. Whatever is real, it is often assumed, can be rationally known, and whatever is rationally known can be con-trolled. So deeply engrained are these assumptions that we readily apply them to history. Thus we speak of *knowing* history and *making* history.

So far as we really think in this fashion, we delude ourselves, for we cannot know history in the way we know physical objects, nor can we make it in the sense of realizing purposes formulated in advance.

One reason why history cannot in any strict sense be an object of knowledge is that human beings cannot be objects of knowledge. A historical event is not an abstraction in the minds of historians; it is a concrete occurrence in the lives of the human beings involved in the event. When we allow ourselves to think that those who live through an event are too close to it to understand it, whereas historians of a later age will be able to view it objectively and in that way to determine what really happened, we are victims of an intellectualist illusion. The greater objectivity of later generations may yield insights unavailable to the participants. But the past is only fragmentarily recovered through such objectivity.

It is only through a certain kind of subjectivity that there is any hope of recovering the past in its fullness; this is the subjectivity by which we imaginatively enter into the experiences of those who lived in the past. Empathy is the primary means by which we establish relations with human beings of former ages. It is legitimate for historians to reconstruct events as only they and their generation can see them; but by doing this they only obscure the past, unless at the same time they reconstruct events as only the participants could have seen them, and unless they realize that the basic truth of the past must be found in the experiences and destinies of the participants.

This does not imply, however, that the historian's only function is that of enabling us to imagine what it was like to live in some earlier time or to take part in a certain series of events. It is widely recognized that by interpreting the past the historian plays a creative role. It is a creative role because it requires going beneath the surface of experience. The function of the historian is not simply to relive the past experience as it has already been lived. He must interpret that experience. In studying a certain period or set of events, he must try to discover what occurred in the inner depths of the human beings who lived in that period or went through those events. Thus the aim of trying to discover "what really happened" is wrong only if it means—as in fact it usually does—trying to work out a complete, objective explanation. But if it means trying to discover what really happened in the innermost being of those who lived in the past, it is altogether legitimate. What we seek in the past is simply the truth. The error in much historical scholarship is to suppose that the truth lies in a factual account or a historical law. The truth is more personal than that. Historiography is a creative task because it calls for construing past experience in order to make clear the personal truth that lies beneath it.

Viewed comprehensively, history of course comprises not only the past but also the future, and here we find another reason why history cannot be an object of knowledge. It is unfinished. This does not mean merely that it is not yet, as a totality, available for study. It means that we are forced into a relationship with history that is unlike any relationship with a mere physical object. History presents us with issues, and it forces us to make decisions. History imposes responsibility, and this responsibility cannot be refused, for even to do nothing is to decide and to bear responsibility.

Historical responsibility is trying because of our weakness. We can no more take history into our possession through action than we can through knowledge. The problem in both cases is man—the being who, as Karl Jaspers remarks, is always more than he can know about himself. Just as man cannot be assuredly known, neither can he be assuredly controlled. It is true that we make history, but we do not make it as we please. It has become particularly apparent in the twentieth century that our ability to calculate the consequences of historical decisions and occurrences is slight. The military and economic reverses that the United States, in spite of all its industrial might, has suffered in recent years lend poignancy to the biblical warning that in the midst of prosperity and success man should beware lest his heart be "lifted up" and he suppose that his good fortune is the fruit of his own wisdom and mastery.[3]

We may infer that any meaning history has is not the kind of objective and demonstrable meaning that belongs to a process established to reach a certain end. It is not just that we lack the understanding to comprehend it as a process or the power to organize it as a process, although

3. The warning against taking deep satisfaction in one's historical condition, lest "thine heart be lifted up, and thou forget the Lord thy God," is contained in Deuteronomy 8:11–14. The principal thinker who applied this warning to America was Reinhold Niebuhr. Works such as *The Irony of American History* (New York: Charles Scribner's Sons, 1952) are particularly trenchant commentaries on naïve American idealism.

that is part of the truth. History is made up of persons, of beings who are essentially more than elements in a process. If history were a process, it would not be a human reality. Thus the very phrase "process of history" is questionable. It suggests that man, in knowledge and action, is more than man; it suggests that man, as the object of knowledge and action, is less than man.

It has been proposed that history may have the kind of meaning that is found in a literary drama, such as a novel or a play. This idea is appealing today because it implies the possibility of finding meaning in even the most tragic and futile history—the kind of history we are living through. On reflection, however, it is plain that the idea must be rejected. We cannot be related to history as we can to a work of art. If the past is a personal mystery to which we are related only by a probing empathy, and if the future requires decisions then history is no more an object of aesthetic contemplation than it is of scientific knowledge and control.

"History in its entirety," asserts Albert Camus, "could only exist in the eyes of an observer outside it and outside the world. History only exists, in the final analysis, for God."[4] History does not exist, then, for man—not history as an object of knowledge, control, or aesthetic contemplation. To say this, however, underscores the question with which we began, that of how we can and should be related to history. Here perhaps the concept of community can help us. The past and the future are personal realities, and to ask how we are related to them is to ask how we are related to human beings who lived in the past and will live in the future. The concept of community suggests that we are related to human beings of the past and the future in the same way in which we are related to human beings in the present—by communication.

This is implicit in the idea that we can understand historical events only by entering into the minds of those who took part in them. I engage in communication when I accord attention to another human being and try to feel and think as he does. This is true even of communication about the most abstract ideas. I must understand those ideas in relation to the situations and passions of human beings. If we were speaking only of face-to-face relationships, all of this would be commonplace. Is

4. Albert Camus, *The Rebel*, trans. Anthony Bower (New York: Alfred A. Knopf, 1954), 256.

it not equally true, however, of historical relationships? If I truly understand the ideas, emotions, and actions of ancient Greeks or medieval Christians, it is by reliving them in my own imagination. It is by putting myself in the place of other people, as I do when communicating face-to-face.

Serious communication, however, probes and inquires. It is not merely a transfer of experience from one mind to another. In talking with someone in my immediate presence, I try to discover not only what that person has thought and felt but also the sources and consequences—and the truth—of those inner states. So it is in attending to past generations, and this is where the creativity of the historian enters into the communicative activity by which we establish relationships with earlier ages. We strive through historical inquiry to put ourselves in the place of those who have lived before us. But we do not wish only to know what they thought and felt; we would like to be clear about things that to them were confused. Thus in studying the American Civil War I would like not only to imagine the feelings of a young man willing to kill and be killed for the sake of the Union or the Confederacy. I would also like to understand what was probably in most cases obscure to the young man: the sources of this willingness. Thus we strive to understand past generations better than they understood themselves—not, however, by objectively explaining what happened to them but by entering more deeply into their experiences than they were able to themselves.

Historiography, then, is not burying the dead but is rather a way of listening to them. Is not communication, however, speaking as well as listening? If so, how can our historical relationships be communal? This brings us to the future. It is true that we cannot speak to the dead, but we can speak to those who are yet to live, and we continually try to do so.

The effort to achieve lasting renown is one way of doing this. But renown is an egoistic motive and is a temptation to deception. It is possible for truth to be a motive in addressing the future. Human beings of one generation may hope that generations to come will perhaps not honor them, but at least not ignore them, not misunderstand them, and not unjustly condemn them. They may accordingly try to leave clear accounts of their deeds and thoughts. In doing this they address and try to establish communal relations with those who are not yet living.

Examples of such communal efforts are the autobiographies and memoirs that public figures often publish at the end of their lives. Most people, of course, rarely think of how the future will see them. But if we were fully to meet the demands of our communal nature, we would frequently, as it were, look back on our lives. We would try to make our lives not only honorable but lucid, not only just and full but transparent to the future.

Further, just as we strive to enter more deeply into the experiences of past generations than they were able to do themselves, we cannot but hope to be better understood by future generations than we understand ourselves. We cannot wish for the darkness and confusion of our lives to be eternal. Hence in addressing the future we do not merely provide factual chronologies. We describe our convictions and emotions, and in doing this, we appeal for understanding. We appeal, as in talking with a friend, for an understanding deeper than our own.

In some measure we can even put ourselves in the place of those addressed in this way—in the place of those who are yet to live. This is admittedly difficult. Social change has become so swift and incalculable that we can scarcely imagine how the world will look to those living a century from now. We cannot put ourselves in the place of future generations even with the limited confidence with which we can put ourselves in the place of past generations. Yet an empathy that reaches into the future is not totally impossible. We can place ourselves in the future insofar as we can imagine our own time not as present but as receding into the past. This means realizing that the issues facing us now will in one way or another be settled and that what confronts us now as an open future will be a congealed reality more or less dimly remembered. We can place ourselves in the future also by realizing that generations then living will be concerned, as are we ourselves, to understand what has gone before. Hence they will be concerned to understand us. By taking deliberate care to help them do this, we establish tenuous communal relationships with them.

In short, what I am suggesting, in place of the objectivity with which it is often supposed we should study history, is "intersubjectivity." People of past generations are not objects of study, nor are those of future generations objects of control; both are subjects, both are beings of a kind to whom we offer, as far as possible, attention and speech. In looking back, rather than trying only to develop theories that explain past events and rather than regarding those events as elements in a process having its whole meaning in our own historical purposes, we manifest our respect for the dead by according them our disinterested attention. We refuse to regard them as mere means to our own ends, and hence we suspend our own purposes in communicative openness. In looking ahead, rather than trying to master the course of events and in that way control those to come, we try to conduct ourselves not only responsibly but also lucidly, so that our lives will speak even when we ourselves are dead. We look on those to come as potential sharers of a truth that encompasses both their times and ours. In sum, our interest in the past and future is expressed in efforts to establish a community comprising all ages and all mankind. The impossibility of doing this with anything remotely approaching complete success does not make the effort less indispensible to our humanity.

These ways of looking at history may seem strange. If so, the main reason, probably, is that we are habituated to thinking of history as something we can know and make. The main ideas that make up a communal view of history are both simple and close to personal experience. We seek friends and acquaintances and care for parents and children because we do not wish to be alone and because we feel we could not really be ourselves if we were forced to be alone; the motives that lead us to study and reflect on history are essentially the same. We cultivate our relationships with those immediately around us through attentiveness and speech; these are also the ways we establish relationships with the historical past and the distant future. In short, the bonds and strategies manifest in our most intimate and selective relationships constitute also our most public and inclusive relationships. If it were compatible with the human situation, I would find intimate friends in every century and place.

It would be well for readers to keep in mind this simple and familiar core in all that has so far been said, for to move ahead it is necessary to touch on a question that, as Karl Löwith remarks, "takes one's breath away." [5] Authentic community is not just casual contact, it is sharing. For conscious beings, sharing is always in some form a sharing of the truth; and since the truth in itself transcends every formulation of the

5. Karl Löwith, *Meaning in History* (Chicago: University of Chicago Press, 1949), 4.

truth, sharing the truth means sharing the search for truth. Even so limited and humble a communal act as sharing a bottle of wine has an inquiring character. This is the case with the sharing that constitutes history. In listening to the past and addressing the future, we search for the truth. For what truth? One great and ultimate question stands in the background of all historical research and reflection—the question of the meaning of history.

The Meaning of History

Most of the questions we ask about history are of course far more limited. In studying the history of Greece, for example, we inquire into the nature and relations of classes within the city-states, and we ask how Athens, with its superior power and energy, came to lose the Peloponnesian War. Many would argue, moreover, that such limits are appropriate. We should confine ourselves to the limited questions, for in principle they are answerable. To ask about the meaning of history is to open the door to illusions and occasionally to bloodshed.

The question, however, is irrepressible, as forbidding as it is. I noted at the outset that our interest in God necessarily prompts us to ask about the meaning of history. But so does our interest in man, our desire to enter into relations with human beings of every time. The significance of our lives is threatened by their subordination to time and to history. Due to this subordination, the human race is dispersed across the ages and every relationship is doomed. Why is this so? Only if we can gain the sense that it is not simply a brute, irrational fact—that history *does* have meaning—can we avoid feeling that our lives ultimately signify nothing. All are subject to this condition, all who live now and all who ever have lived or will live.

Accordingly, every reason why we cannot follow the advice of Kierkegaard and turn away from history is a reason also why we cannot ignore the question of the meaning of history. Those whom I love and would know as fully as possible are products of the whole past of mankind, and the meaning of their lives is affected by what happens in the most distant future; I would know them fully only if I knew the meaning of history. As for the multitudes who have lived and died and who are yet to live, I share with all of them a common condition—subjection to the alienating force of time and the passage of generations; to look for meaning in this condition is to look for a Logos uniting all human beings. Finally, I inquire into history to see whether the apparent hostility of time toward every present relationship is as implacable as it seems; that too means asking about the meaning of history. For all of these reasons, the truth that we seek in history concerns the meaning of history. Only this truth would clarify fully our lives and open the way to community.

Consequently, in studying a subject like ancient Athens, questions more comprehensive and perplexing than the kind that historians usually ask will cross our minds. For example, has a people ever come nearer to community than did the Athenians in Periclean times? If not, if gains like the abolition of slavery have been counterbalanced by losses like the rise of bureaucracy, what has been accomplished in the intervening millennia? Does everything that man achieves necessarily pass away completely?

Looking into the future, such questions are apt to be more pressing and more unpleasant. In this case we must think of ourselves as dead and we must think of our own achievements as having receded into the mists of memory. Can we do this without feeling that our lives and efforts are cursed with futility?

It is especially our mortality, as individuals and as societies and civilizations, that forces us to consider the meaning of history. When I try to enter into the lives of those now dead and when I think of myself and my own generation as dead, I cannot help being struck by the apparent vanity of our lives. We seem to be part of an endless and inexorable procession into the past and into final oblivion. What is worth caring about? What or whom can we care about without involving ourselves in certain tragedy? The meaning of history is not merely an academic question. It is not the sort of question that we can ignore if it does not happen to interest us.

It must be emphasized, however, that seeking the meaning of history is not something different and apart from the empirical investigation of history. It is rather the form that historical inquiry, beginning as empirical investigation, must assume if pursued to the end. The chasm dividing the philosophy of history from ordinary historical scholarship in the universities is owing to the difficulty that any single mind has in grasping both ultimate meaning and immediate facts; but it has nothing to do with the reality studied, for that is one. A good empirical historian wants not merely to piece together the facts but also to discover the ultimate meaning of the facts. A philosopher of history, on the other hand, is not looking for a scheme that leaves the facts untouched but rather for one that makes it possible for the facts to be truly understood.

It is apparent why, in turning to the meaning of history, we have not left behind our concern with entering into the lives of those who have lived or have yet to live. If we could discern the ultimate meaning of history, we would possess a key to the inner life of every person who has ever lived or is yet to live. There is an enormous misunderstanding involved when the philosophy of history issues in a vast, impersonal scheme unrelated and threatening to individuals. The meaning of history is the inner meaning of individual lives. We began this discussion by looking at history as a set of occurrences in the lives of concrete human beings; we construed the effort to understand these occurrences as communication. This communicative effort would reach its culmination if we could understand the significance of all that has ever happened for every human being who has ever lived. This would be the truth, the fully personal truth, that we look for in the past and the future.

But how can we presume to entertain so overwhelming a question as that of the meaning of history? We cannot, if we are looking for objective knowledge or for a solution of the sort that will permanently dispose of the question. If history is not something we can know, control, or contemplate, then it cannot be assigned any literal and demonstrable meaning. It does not follow, however, that history is meaningless.

For one thing, history provides intimations of meaning. These intimations are not in the nature of information or knowledge; they tell us nothing *about* the past or future. But they come to us with persuasive persistence and force. Generation after generation has felt that something of ultimate significance came to expression in Periclean Athens; people again and again have sensed anomalous hints of eternity in the Rome of Julius Caesar and Augustus; Americans have been increasingly aware in their own Civil War of mysterious overtones of destiny. If we try to translate such intuitions into explicit, factual propositions they often evaporate, leaving us with nothing but dead and implausible words. But they do offer assurance that thinking about the meaning of history is not senseless.

Further, it is possible to think and speak without using words in literal ways. It is not easy to do this, but it is indispensable if we are to inquire and communicate concerning realities that are not mere matters of fact. Thus it is possible to consider history as if it were an objectively knowable series of events spread out before us in their entirety, bearing in mind all the while that it is not a matter of fact but is rather a mystery that encompasses all matters of fact and is irreducible to objective form. It is possible to speak ostensibly about the shape of history while being concerned in reality with the orientation of human beings within history. It is possible, finally, to offer as though for the intellect alone what is in truth an appeal to the whole intuitive being of historical man.

These are the tactics, it seems to me, of an indispensable duplicity. Without them we would be reduced to thoughtlessness and silence before matters of the greatest moment. To be sure that our duplicity remains beneficent, however, we must resolutely maintain the sovereignty of communication. I suspect that Marxism became destructive because it became an *explanation* of community rather than a matter for inquiring communication and in that way a *bond* of community. We must keep our ideas about history in a context of open and unfinished dialogue. In this way, rather than congealing into dogmas in the name of which others are oppressed, they may call forth communal relations.

This approach may be illustrated through some of the principal theories of historical meaning. Most ancient thinkers, and a few recent thinkers, have viewed history as cyclical. The past supposedly returns, again and again. As a statement of fact, such a theory can have little standing. Times demonstrably change; and if we could know what is coming, that very knowledge would be a new element in the situation, altering the cycle and falsifying the theory. As a metaphor, however, the cyclical conception is worth considering. It is a way, for example, of affirming an underlying and eternal order, an order comprising both nature and human affairs. With confidence in the indefeasible reality of an order of this kind, one may withstand the crushing force of events. Such an attitude can be discerned in Plato, who lived through the declining years of the Greek *polis*. Alternatively, the cyclical conception can be understood as an assertion of the futility of history. As such, it calls on us to take neither human achievements nor human failures with unqualified seriousness. This view can be found in Ecclesiastes. In opposition to both of these views, however, it may be argued that cyclical interpretations invariably reduce history to something unbearably inane and thus encourage political irresponsibility. In the balance, what should one think?

Augustine and other Christians have set forth an eschatological vision in which history moves toward a catastrophic end, after which man inhabits the transhistorical realms symbolized as Heaven and Hell. History does not continue everlastingly but finally, like a vast wave, deposits human life beyond the torrents of time. This could not be literally true. How could the end of history be a historical event? What, then, does it mean? Is it a way of attributing significance to history while asserting the finitude and imperfection of all governments, churches, and other historical entities? Is it a way of ascribing to man a splendor so great that finally the very conditions of historical existence must be shattered? Or does it drain history of all meaning (was not Augustine basically indifferent to the fall of Rome?) and undermine our respect for the small-scale satisfactions and arrangements that are the stuff of daily life?

Today we can hardly avoid reflecting on a third conception of history—the doctrine of progress. During the eighteenth and nineteenth centuries, collective life was interpreted and guided largely in terms of this doctrine. Revolution and industrialization, for example, thus gained what seemed rational sanction. But suddenly, under the impact of the disasters that began to unfold in 1914, the idea of progress as normal and natural lost its plausibility. The result is a crisis in our understanding of the universe and our place in it. Hence we must ask questions such as whether the doctrine of progress encourages a salutary confidence in the course of affairs or only obscures the power and persistence of evil. Could it be that progress comes about through failure— for example, spiritual progress through political and economic failure? If there is not progress of any kind, can history have any meaning?

In discussing these conceptions of history—the cyclical, the eschatological, and the progressive—we inquire into the significance of our collective existence in time. This is the question of all questions. If we knew the meaning of history, we would know the meaning of our existence and would dwell in the truth.

But we must not forget the nature of this inquiry. For one thing, it is more personal than it looks. Ostensibly concerned with historical forces in comparison with which individuals are seemingly nothing, it is really concerned with personal life—with what makes it significant and with how it should be borne in view of the historical uncertainties and misfortunes to which it is exposed. And we must not forget that the truth lies in the inner certainties of communal man and not in any objective theory. History is most dangerous when it is supposedly comprehended. Any interpretation of history is inhumane if it takes the form of an ideology. When inquiring into history, therefore, we look for insights of a kind that do not constitute a conclusion or bring inquiry to an end. In sum, thinking about the meaning of history should not be a voyage among vast abstractions; it should bring us nearer to concrete persons.

Some readers, however, may protest so much emphasis on inquiry and communication. They may assert that history is primarily a matter of action, not of inquiry. History occurs because human beings face problems on which they must act. It would be difficult wholly to disagree. But how can the necessity of action be reconciled with the communal conception of history so far sketched?

Action and History

We are not asking about any kind of action whatever. We are asking about *historical* action, and that means politics. Although man is a historical being and not a political being in some nonhistorical sense (as in Aristotle), he is historical through politics.

This may seem questionable. Why should one form of action—politics—be designated as the historical form? In a broad sense, every human act is historical, for history is the entire story of the past. Even a trivial act on the part of an ordinary person may be of interest to a historian as a manifestation of the life of the age in which that person lived. A significant act by a powerful person, an act appreciably affecting the course of events, may seem more definitely historical; it absolutely compels the attention of historians. Yet neither act is necessarily historical in that neither is necessarily a conscious effort to influence the course of history. It is the conscious effort to affect events that determines the historical character of an act. If *accidentally* affecting events could make an act historical, then an animal, such as the horse that threw Stonewall Jackson and rendered him unconscious during a critical period before a pending battle, would be capable of a historical act; if *successfully* trying to affect events were the criterion of the historical, a statesman like Woodrow Wilson trying in vain to link the United States with League of Nations might be *in*capable of a historical act. An act is historical, then, if motivated by a concern for the overall, the historical state of man.

Politics is simply the conduct of common affairs; it involves in essence the comprehensive concern that lies at the source of historical action. It is not that history is actually controlled through politics. It is rather that through politics we assume (or try to assume, as in running for office) that socially recognized responsibility for common affairs, for the course of historical events, that falls to government. This does not imply that historical action depends on holding public office, but only that it depends on the kind of sustained and comprehensive consideration of the overall state of society that is the normal responsibility of those who do hold office.

Here we reach an important juncture in these reflections. Politics entails the attempt to understand man's historical situation. Political leaders try to characterize prevailing circumstances in public addresses; commissions are established to study particular problems; parliaments and cabinets debate various possible interpretations of existing conditions. In short, a great deal of inquiring communication takes place. Politics entails a serious search for the truth. What is sought, moreover, is truth about history—usually only about a particular historical situation, but occasionally, as with Abraham Lincoln, about the meaning of history. Why? How does it happen that politics becomes involved in the process of historical inquiry that has been our concern throughout these reflections?

At first glance, the answer seems obvious: for the sake of effective action. But is that answer as adequate as it seems? It is certainly not entirely without validity. It expresses a practical necessity, that of needing understanding in order to act effectively; and it expresses a common norm, one deriving from a preoccupation with action and a consequent tendency to assume that understanding is valuable only so far as it is useful. Does it, however, express a reasonable norm? From the vantage point gained in this essay we are bound to question any proposition that, even implicitly, justifies historical inquiry in terms of practical utility. In the first place, the practical utility of our historical understanding is relatively slight. Since history is not an object of action and cannot be deliberately controlled, politics in its larger undertakings is bound to be more or less unsuccessful. Such a notion is drastically at odds with modern man's self-confidence, but history in general, and recent history in particular, abounds in evidence that supports it. In the second place, understanding history is, as we have seen, valuable in itself. Despite Marx, the point is not to change the world. At least, that is not the *whole* point.

These considerations enable us to look at action in an unaccustomed way. They indicate that it is not enough to say that we try to understand in order to act. We must also say that we act in order to understand. In acting we probe into the structures of reality and we experiment with our own ambitions and desires. We find out more about the world and about ourselves. Since we are unlikely to achieve fully the results envisioned at the outset, and since understanding is of worth in itself, it would be erroneous to regard what we learn in the course of action as having only trivial or instrumental value. Of course action would not be action if it did not aim at a result other than truth. But the genuine success of an action, it appears, must be measured partly by a result that it does not aim at—enhanced understanding.

This suggests that politics should be viewed as a form of inquiry as well as a form of action. And if inquiry is carried on through communication—through parliamentary debates, cabinet discussions, and the like—and if inquiry and communication in their most serious forms are identical, then we may say that politics is an aspect of the communal activity through which we enter into history. The final goal of politics is always something beyond the sum of immediate practical effects envisioned in connection with a particular political undertaking. That goal is a common understanding of history and its meaning.

Past and future generations are readily brought into politics as an inquiring and communal activity. Political leaders are spontaneously historical, almost always placing their actions in a sequence with past actions. Franklin Roosevelt saw the New Deal as a continuation of the policies of Woodrow Wilson and Theodore Roosevelt; several generations of Communist leaders have envisioned themselves as heirs of the Paris Commune. Such sequences, moreover, are not normally confined to those who agree. Roosevelt saw his administration as a departure from the laissez-faire administrations that immediately preceded it, and it is essential in the self-conception of Communists that they are successors to capitalists (although they never are). Sequential views of this sort, of course, are often shallow or dogmatic; almost always they are self-congratulatory. Nevertheless, they reflect at least rudimentary historical communities; present leaders place themselves in the company of past leaders.

They place themselves no less persistently in the company of future leaders. From the latter they hope at best for emulation and at least for understanding. A political leader is scarcely responsible if he does not think of what he is doing for the future, and that is to look at what he is doing through the eyes of the future. As noted, the idea of communicating with the unborn sounds strange but is a commonplace political concern.

The wisdom of not counting on political success has been clearly shown by the tribulations of our time. Political activity is deluded unless attended by a readiness for failure—not for total failure, perhaps, but for something far short of success. This is made apparent by practically every great political undertaking of our times—by the wars, with their aftermath of disorder and despair; by the revolutions, leading almost invariably to despotism; by the efforts to establish economic justice, which have yet to prove their feasibility. Politics would be unendurably futile unless it had a purpose distinct from immediate purposes and capable of being fulfilled even when immediate purposes are not fulfilled. That purpose, I am suggesting, is common—that is, communal and inquiring—insight into our historical situation and into the meaning of history.

As it happens, failure in action often deepens our understanding. It destroys proud illusions concerning our power and wisdom and invites reflection. Thus politics may be fruitful as a mode of inquiry when it is frustrating as a mode of action. It marks a signal misunderstanding of leadership when a government pursues a vain enterprise, as did the United States government in Vietnam, on the grounds that giving it up would be intolerably disappointing for the governed. The task of political leadership is not just to organize programs of action that succeed but to help show how people should bear themselves when those programs do not succeed.

The concept of politics as a mode of inquiring communication implies that we should act in a spirit of inaction. The ideal of detachment in the midst of action is a major theme of the Bhagavad-Gita. What is called for—both by the concept I am suggesting and by the Hindu classic—is a state of self-transcendence in which we seek certain results but do so realizing that the ultimate value of the seeking will not be wholly decided by the results actually obtained. One of the major qualifications for political leadership is the capacity for refraining from total commitment to one's own purposes and designs. This capacity may be evident in a sense of humor; Adlai Stevenson is a lustrous example. It may be evident also in a willingness to engage in political inquiry, for a leader who acts in a spirit of inaction is not afraid for his decisions and plans to be subjected to rational examination.

Conceived of in this way, politics is an important, but not destructive, activity. It is important because it serves, as no other activity does, the enterprise of conscious participation in history. Man is a political being because he is a historical being.

Politics is not destructive when conceived of as a mode of inquiring communication, because it is freed from the passion for historical mastery. It is inherent in the very idea of participation—of being part—that one accepts the inconclusiveness of his own actions. Hence to aim at participating in history is to aim not at historical ascendancy but at a certain sort of historical immanence. Pretensions of being more than human are given up. Further, if I aim at participating through listening and speaking, I recognize that not only am I not *more* than human, but that others are not *less*.

Ever since the time of the French Revolution, modern man has displayed a strong desire to gain historical sovereignty. He has repeatedly wagered everything on results. Some of the worst moments in history have ensued. Lenin is probably the most dramatic example of the modern preoccupation with results. The incivility of Lenin himself and of the regime he established came partly as a consequence of this preoccupation. If nothing matters but results, freedom is indefensible except as a provisional arrangement. It must be abolished, as it was early in Soviet history, when it seems to be in the way of governmental designs.

The passion for mastery not only arouses a pride that is destructive to freedom, but it necessarily gives rise to doubts about popular participation in politics. The problem is not simply that a government in which the general populace takes part may be less efficient than one in which power is highly concentrated, although that is part of the problem. Thinking purely in terms of results, it is hard to explain to the average citizen why, as merely one of millions, one should bother with politics. The political activities of millions of citizens combined may, of course, have substantial historical consequences; and a few from out of these multitudes will reach positions of unusual influence. But the average citizen feels with good reason that he himself, as a single individual, can have only a negligible effect in public affairs—which is to say, on the course of history. In the democracies, those who try to inspire widespread participation in elections often are driven to the desperate expedient of suggesting that the outcome of an election may be decided by a single vote. This absurdity shows how preoccupied we are with results and how impossible it is, on those terms, to provide a reasonable justification for voting. The average person cannot be made to believe that by voting or by engaging in political activity in any other way, he can significantly affect the course of history. What he can, and should, be persuaded to believe, however, is that by political activity he may become a participant in his times and in history and that he responds in this way to the demands of his own universality.

All of this has a bearing on the political polarities facing us in the twentieth century. The assumption that politics is a mode of action and nothing more gives rise to ideologies, formulae for human sovereignty. The idea that politics is a mode not only of action but also of inquiring communication offers a possible standpoint beyond the ideologies.

Conservatism, Radicalism, and Historical Continuity

Under the imperative of universality, we must respect both past and future, and this means accepting a standard that is neither conservative nor radical—that of continuity. The past is not to be lost, the present neglected, nor the future repudiated. This is not to prescribe three different tasks, however, but one—that of trying to enter into relations with all mankind. Time ceaselessly resists our doing this, and our victories are never more than partial and temporary. But we would jeopardize our very humanity if we did not as far as possible dispute the right of death and the passage of generations to sever our links with one another.

While the enmity of time is unremitting, however, it varies in intensity. There are periods when time seems overwhelming, and efforts to counter its corrosive force are feeble and ineffective. We ourselves, I believe, live in such a period. Even the recent past, with its strange machines and dress, seems quaint and distant. The future is almost totally obscured; we try to envision it in fantasies that sometimes depict worldly paradise and sometimes forecast scientific despotism or nuclear annihilation. No doubt technology, with the sudden, unforeseen changes it causes, has contributed to this condition. But the power of technology reflects on man's part a willing subservience (Joseph Wood Krutch remarks that whenever the immediate application of some new invention is proposed, the response is, "Hold on to your hats, boys, here we go!"[6]), and this may be owing to a prior disorientation in time. In any case, the present has become a narrow ridge, dropping away abruptly on either side.

This situation is reflected in recent political attitudes. In any society there are bound to be differences of opinion concerning the most desirable rate of historical change. The tension between radicalism and conservatism is endemic in historical existence. But each of these in recent times has become a total and exclusive viewpoint, betokening a failure to come to terms with time. The past has been treated with contempt, as in both the French and Soviet revolutions. It has been interpreted as primarily a succession of crimes and exploitative acts from which man had violently to disengage himself. The standard of humanity lay in commitment to the future. Countering this attitude and the actions expressing it was an impassioned reaffirmation of the past. Recoiling from the future, opponents of revolution prescribed as the primary duty of

6. Joseph Wood Krutch, *Human Nature and the Human Condition* (New York: Random House, 1959), 144.

statesmen the preservation or reestablishment of old institutions, traditions, and outlooks. The key to being human was found in loyalty to the past.

By thus mutilating history, both radicals and conservatives have sustained a measure of worldly optimism. This is not obvious in the case of conservatives, who frequently denounce historical optimism as a failing of the radical mind. In his more unguarded moments, however, Edmund Burke counted no less on historical possibilities than did his revolutionary opponents. He differed from them primarily in his strategy; he saw historical success as dependent on caution and on respect for the past. Consequently he differed from them in his conception of community, which was more a sharing of traditions than of creative activity, more aristocratic than egalitarian, more disciplined than spontaneous. Burke was as inspired as any radical, however, by the vision of worldly community. He was far from recognizing the tragic character of history. Hegel, not speaking as the conservative he sometimes is held to have been, wrote that history "forms a picture of most fearful aspect, and excites emotions of the profoundest and most hopeless sadness."[7] This remark mirrors the attitudes of early Christian writers such as Augustine, who saw history as beginning in sin and estrangement, as unfolding through bitter tensions and upheavals, and as ending in the destruction of the world. In comparison with views such as these, both conservatism and radicalism seem decidedly optimistic.

The strategies by which this optimism is sustained, moreover, in both cases are equally questionable. We cannot live in history by assigning most of the evils of historical existence to, and then making it the task of politics to suppress, either the past or the future. It is not just that bloodshed and injustice are likely to follow, although they are. Through such strategies historical continuity, the all-inclusive community of man, is disrupted. Participation in history is precluded. Not that participation in history is the primary goal of either conservatives or radicals. Their primary goal is historical mastery, to be attained either through duplicating the past in the future, at least approximately, or through severing the past from the future and abandoning it completely. These are the conservative and radical strategies, respec-

7. Georg Wilhelm Friedrich Hegel, *The Philosophy of History*, trans. J. Sibree (Rev. ed.; New York: Willey Book Co., no date), 21.

tively, for controlling historical time. But in truth people employing these strategies succumb to time, for at the very outset they give up the possibility of a participatory and communal relationship with a major segment of history—the future, in the case of the conservatives, and the past, in the case of radicals. And they devote themselves less to communication than to action.

The concept of historical continuity is only a restatement of the central theme we have reached in this set of reflections. Continuity is achieved through communication, through being attentive to the past, and through rendering our lives as an address to the future. Inquiring unreservedly, we inquire into all times, and we not only inquire *about* human beings of all times but also *with* them. Past ages speak explicitly through their literature and art, and implicitly through their actions. We do not owe the men of these ages enshrinement in unchallengeable traditions, but only critical attention. In turn what we say and do can be an address to the future. Just as we respect but do not revere those who lived in the past, so we should speak and act in relation to the future as human beings and not as gods legislating for all time or as beasts who have no historical future. This means living with the awareness that we are not voicing truths and setting patterns of life that will divest coming ages of either the right or the duty to have their own contests with obscurity and chaos. It means striving not to achieve changeless perfection, but to do things worth remembering, to be articulate, and to preserve conditions in which civilized memory in centuries to come will be possible.

If we could participate in history as though it were an inquiry of centuries and millennia, we would be less tempted than we are to divide and distort the historical sequence. Participants in inquiry are interested both in all that has been said and in all that may yet be said, and they are unwilling ever to smother inquiry in conclusions. In the Socratic circle, past conversations were remembered and perhaps often rehearsed. While Socrates was living, however, new conversations frequently occurred; and Socrates never allowed himself to think, even in the hours immediately before his death, that answers had been established in a way that precluded further inquiry.[8] A person might participate in history with similar attitudes, with critical interest both in what has gone

8. See Plato, *Phaedo*, trans. R. Hackforth (Cambridge: Cambridge University Press, 1972).

before and in what is yet to come, resisting every program designed forcibly to bring the course of events to a conclusion.

Would this not, however, be to accept the indefinite continuance of evil and injustice? It would; and to feel for this reason serious misgivings about the whole idea of historical continuity is not inappropriate. To say anything except that evil must be opposed and so far as possible destroyed is dangerous. It corresponds neatly with the desire of the privileged (including practically every writer) to find some moral sanction for acquiescing in the injustices suffered by others.

Nevertheless, in the lives of individuals—to say nothing for the moment of societies—suffering cannot be wholly eliminated. Moreover, through suffering may come spiritual growth. At least these are axioms of a common wisdom. Misfortunes are not simply to be forgotten as quickly as possible, nor are they merely to be studied in the hope of avoiding them in the future. For one who endures and remembers them, they provide a way toward a deeper and fuller humanity.

Is it otherwise with societies? The denial of continuity, especially on the radical side, often seems to come from the assumption that evil can be largely excluded from history. But a way must be found of acknowledging, without complacency or callousness, that probably it cannot. And we must take into account, in social and political philosophy, that a people probably cannot come near to being a true community without living through and remembering historical tragedies. These disclose its mortal condition and its human fallibility, and for some they hint of the God at whose wrath "the earth shall tremble" and whose indignation "the nations shall not be able to abide." [9] The American Civil War, for example, on the surface was a vast and unnecessary act of fratricide. But Americans are increasingly absorbed in a kind of national meditation on this tragedy. They seem to sense in it meanings that they cannot clearly formulate, but by virtue of which the United States is a more substantial community now than it would have been without this catastrophic failure of community in its past.

It would be an understatement to say that the realization of continuity is difficult. As anything but a fragmentary and ephemeral achievement, it is impossible. We hear only broken, occasional, obscure utterances from the past, and we feel no assurance that the future will

9. Jeremiah 10:10

attend to the words and acts of the present. The standard of continuity poses the strange and seemingly hopeless task of transmuting all of history into dialogue.

But the very effort, if widely practiced, would tend to deepen our common life. To aim at continuity is to observe each of the principles that have emerged from these reflections: to acknowledge that man cannot be indifferent to any part of history, to recognize that history is mysterious and not to be managed; to approach the past and the future in an inquiring and communal, rather than proud, frame of mind; and to do all of this even in the midst and by means of action. This is to aim simply at being civil, at entering into the company of all humanity. We can hardly ask less of ourselves.

VIII / COMMUNITY AND FAITH

Does community depend in any way on religious faith, or is it a purely natural phenomenon? This question is of theoretical interest since it concerns the roots of human relations. It is of more than theoretical interest, however, in view of the apparent fact that faith in our time is weak and growing weaker.

Our views in this matter have drastically changed. A few hundred years ago it was everywhere assumed that the unity of man and man depended on the unity of man and God. The religious fragmentation brought by the Reformation jeopardized, in the eyes of many, not only true faith but community as well. Today completely different assumptions prevail. For some, community and faith are in conflict. Even believers generally take it for granted that sound relationships between human beings do not depend on religious faith.

It is not only liberals who evince such views. Marxists, for example, do so as well. Faith is not unnecessary to community as Marxists see it; it is actually antithetical to community. It diverts men—or expresses a diversion effected by the economic system—from the revolutionary task of abolishing alienation here on earth. Only as human beings rise into full consciousness of their sovereignty in a godless universe will they establish real communities. A character in one of Dostoevsky's novels (expressing an attitude that Dostoevsky himself did not share) asserts that the concept of personal immortality is disappearing and that in consequence "the immense reserves of love that were lavished on Him who *was* immortality are now directed toward nature, the world, fellow men, every blade of grass." [1] Broadly this expresses the modern attitude—an attitude seldom questioned.

1. Fyodor Dostoevsky, *The Adolescent*, trans. Andrew R. MacAndrew (New York: Doubleday & Co., 1971), 489.

Yet a glance at recent history must give us pause. Common sense may tell us that as the image of God grows faint, our love and respect for one another will increase. But it would be difficult to maintain that this, in fact, is what has happened. On the contrary, human conflict has, in this era of religious doubt, surpassed in ferocity almost every historical precedent. It may be granted that community has been sought with greater passion than ever before. Socialism, communism, and fascism all have aimed at community, diversely defined. To say that community has evaded our grasp, however, would be an understatement. Not only do our wars, by their scale and frequency, indicate how divided we are; even at peace, judging from an immense literature on alienation, we feel separated from one another by vast and untraversable distances.

Moreover, although these failures may seem strange to modern man in his secular self-confidence, loss of faith provides a possible explanation for them. Respect for the individual must be a major prerequisite of community; without such respect, society is bound to sanctify various forms of oppression and exclusion. Yet nothing so exalts the individual as does the idea of his immortality and of the omnipotent God who is interested in his particular destiny. How can the individual be comparably dignified if there is no immortality and no God? And if the individual is not somehow dignified, what will become of community?

This hypothesis is apt to be annoying to agnostics and unbelievers. It may seem that their capacity for community is being challenged. If this were so, they could not be blamed for feeling resentful. The truth is, of course, that skeptics and atheists have been at least as actively and effectively communal as those on the other side. But is faith, or its absence, so definite and plain a fact as we often assume? Some, whose faith is untested, presumably have less faith than they think they have. Do some have more? Can there be such a thing as a tacit faith? The relations of individuals and transcendence may be far more mysterious, and related far more paradoxically to outward religious commitments and even to inward convictions, than either believers or unbelievers normally suppose.

Arguments linking community and faith are also likely to be unwelcome to many people because they seem to raise old and bloody institutional problems now happily behind us. But such is not necessarily the case. Rethinking the relations of community and faith does not mean considering a return to the priestly government of the Middle Ages; it does not mean in any way rejoining state and church. Faith may underlie community, but I suggest that it underlies freedom as well.

In reflecting on the implications of modern secularism, a logical starting point is the general state of man as a secular being—that is, as an object of experience and awareness.

Human Groundlessness

Man exists without reason, without settled identity, and without clear moral justification. This is the state of man so far as we can tell by relying on experience and excluding faith, and this is what I mean by "groundlessness." Such a view is, of course, common in recent thought. Its implications for community, however, have received relatively little attention. Let us briefly examine the various aspects of groundlessness and then consider these implications.

Man exists without reason in the sense that he has not chosen to be in the world and does not see any clear reason why he should be. However accustomed one is to existing, still it is as though one has just happened upon himself. Existing as I do in my own particular circumstances is a mute and arbitrary fact. Many elements within existence can be rationally explained by being traced back to prior causes and choices. But existence itself is inexplicable. No reference to biological causes or parental and ancestral choices enables me to eliminate the strangeness that encompasses my being. I am not the ground of my own being and I am not familiar with that ground. I am, as Martin Heidegger says, "thrown" into the world.[2]

I am also, however, without a settled identity. My mere existence may be a fact, but I myself in my full personal being am not a fact—not, at least, if we think of a fact as something established and self-contained. A fact simply is what it is. The self, however, lacks this definite self-identical character. I am not only the self that I happen upon but also the one who happens upon this self. I can reflect upon, alter, even destroy myself. Thus happening on oneself is not exactly like finding something of definite character and measurable value, such as a coin in the

---

2. See Martin Heidegger, *Being and Time*, trans. John Macquarrie and Edward Robinson (New York: Harper & Row, 1962).

street. The self is encountered as an unexpected question: what shall I be? Man's groundlessness is manifest in the silence of the universe before this question. The nearest we come to discovering a person's settled identity is through a biography written after the subject has lost his worldly being in death.

These two aspects of groundlessness can be summed up as factuality and indeterminacy. One is a verdict of experience, the other of awareness. I happen on myself as on an article that someone else has mislaid or discarded; and I can in turn mislay or discard that self.

A third, and final, aspect of groundlessness consists in lacking clear moral justification. One cannot conscientiously accept the self that he has come upon. This is one of the oldest and most persistent convictions in the history of moral thought. Plato, for example, distinguished between man as he is in existence and as he is in essence, and Aristotle between actual man and potential man. Christianity sharply opposed man in his fallen state and man redeemed. And not only religious thinkers have found the ordinary self unacceptable. Nietzsche denounced the man of nineteenth-century bourgeois civilization and called for a being who would be more than human, the Superman; Marx described the process by which human beings were dispossessed and malformed by capitalism and invoked a vision of cooperative and creative humanity; and even someone as skeptical and austere as Freud presupposed in all of his writings the distinction between the divided and the integrated personality. The whole history of thought is filled with expressions of man's dissatisfaction with himself. For Ortega y Gasset the lack of such dissatisfaction is the crucial characteristic of the degenerate human type constituting the masses.

It may seem that factuality and indeterminacy are more purely negative than moral unacceptability, which seems to presuppose a standard and a source of moral judgment. But all involve a lack—in the two former states a lack of clear reason for being and of established identity, in the latter state a lack of moral authorization. All in this way express groundlessness. And all, by implication, point to a real or hypothetical ground.

We are not concerned with groundlessness as a general problem, however, but with its significance for human relations. How does it bear on the problem of community?

Shame and the Risk of Address

In spite of groundlessness, one must nevertheless stand and act. It is necessary to be someone as though one's reason for being were clearly known. It is necessary to be someone in the midst of uncertainty as to who one is. It is necessary to be a self that is bound to be a source of deep and continuing dissatisfaction. Suicide is no escape from the incongruities of selfhood. It is as incongruous as any other act of self-affirmation. It requires a judgment that personal existence is purposeless, although that is no more justified by natural knowledge than the judgment that it has a particular purpose. It requires that one assume a certain identity, that of a suicide, even though every personal identity must by the standards of natural knowledge be arbitrary. And it requires a determination of personal worth that one is in no position to make. As Dostoevsky brings out through Kirilov, in *The Possessed*, suicide is the act of a man-god.

Personal being, then, in itself and apart from all accidents, is a source of suffering. This is not only because it is incongruous, however. It is also because it must be maintained under the gaze of others. This is an ontological necessity, in that personal existence is inescapably carried on with and subject to the inspection of others; it is a moral necessity, in that becoming a self is subject to the communal imperative that genuine selfhood requires availability to others. But this is to be exposed in all of one's incongruous being. One has to take a position that is ultimately without reason, necessity, or justification, and he must do this in the sight of others. Groundlessness is a social condition. The suffering that comes from the exposure of one's groundlessness is what I understand by shame. The whole situation is dramatized in a biblical myth. Adam and Eve, having become estranged from God, discovered that they were naked, and they were ashamed.

Society manifests our fear of shame. It provides us with a variety of disguises and retreats; dress, manners, rank, and private homes all can serve these functions. As Rousseau and others have bitterly pointed out, these deepen estrangement even if they do offer protection from some of its most painful effects. But one who ignores them seems "shameless"—blind to man's groundlessness and his horror of exposure. Some of the impulses most prominent in the daily life of any society can probably be traced back to shame. The impulse to conform is an example. By conforming one attains the invisibility of being indistinguishable from everyone else. It might seem that no one would seek power and fame. But these ordinarily expose only an artificial public personality, and they may in addition bring an illusion of having risen above the common human state of groundlessness. A tyrant tries to maintain this illusion by suppressing all criticism and opposition.

It is apparent that shame is in some way antagonistic to community. In what way, precisely? This question requires careful consideration.

The crucial communal acts are those of addressing and according attention to other persons. It is in relation to these acts, therefore, that we must look for the effects of shame. These effects are particularly clear in the act of address. To try to express oneself, however casually and informally, is to stand forth from the protective anonymity and uniformity of society. It is also, where the act of address is a genuine appeal to free intelligence, to abandon any ascendancy by which a certain response might be guaranteed. In short, address is exposure. It invites the other person to accord attention and then, by responding, to take a similar risk. But the other person may be unwilling to do either of these things, and one then is exposed to his gaze and judgment. Through an act of address, one implies that the person addressed is not merely an object of experience and appraisal. But one whose address is rejected finds suddenly that he himself is such an object. Being ignored, rather than actively rejected, is a variation on this experience, for one of the main characteristics of a mere object, as distinguished from a person, is that it may legitimately be left aside and accorded no attention.

An act of address, then, necessarily means running a risk. It may seem that an offer of attention is far safer, for a state of attention is comparatively passive and inconspicuous. This is perhaps true. Yet the difficulties of communication would be obscured were all risks assumed to lie on the side of address and none on the side of attention. An effective offer of attention has to be expressed, if only by a smile or a frown. For this to occur, the attention offered must be genuine; if it is merely affected, serious communication is apt to expose it as such. But a state of genuine attention is not easily attained. It requires interest and understanding; and, hardest of all, it requires humility, because without humility one cannot sincerely listen. All of these must be expressed, and there are multiple opportunities for failure. Hence to be addressed is to be an object of certain expectations and thus to suffer a kind of exposure. A failure to respond can bring a feeling of shame not unlike that to which one is vulnerable in an act of address.

There are various ways of withholding address and attention, and thus of escaping the risks involved, without seeming timid or misanthropic and without being embarrassed. One may seek self-sufficiency by habituating oneself to the most accessible and harmless pleasures. This was the prescription of the Epicureans when the main communal form of antiquity, the *polis*, collapsed. Another fortress into which people have often withdrawn when community seemed impossible is that of uncompromising moral rectitude. Here the goal is personal independence based on caring only for what is right. This was the ideal of ancient Stoicism. Both Epicureanism and Stoicism are austere philosophies, requiring severe self-discipline and promising only sombre satisfactions. Both promise freedom from the risks of communication through an ethic founded on an exclusive concern—in one case pleasure, in the other rectitude.

Today, and perhaps in other times as well, the most common refuge from the risks of communication is that of playing a role in society. This means entering into human relationships, since roles are defined by the attitudes of others; fulfilling a social role is incompatible with the self-sufficiency offered by Epicureanism and Stoicism. But the relationships involved in merely conforming with expectations are not truly communal. They do not impose the risks of address and attention, but rather enable one to withdraw behind the screen of an impersonal function.

Epicureanism and Stoicism are both appealing ideals in times like the present when the truth is remote, social tensions are profound, and the risks of communication are thus formidable. They offer not only safety but patterns of life not wholly lacking in dignity. As for playing a role in society, many in this way lead lives that are not only protected from the dangers of address and attention but are useful and honorable.

Every way of evading the risks of communication, however, expresses either pride or self-abandonment—making too much of oneself or too little. And every such way is an acceptance of estrangement. The key to both Epicureanism and Stoicism is pride, the aspiration totally to control one's life—a relatively restrained and harmless pride, perhaps, but pride nevertheless. Acceptance of estrangement is implicit even in the Stoic conception of mankind as a universal city. Each person stands apart, sufficient unto himself in the dispassionate legality of a global citizenship. Fulfilling an established social function expresses the opposite of pride, self-abandonment. The responsibility of deciding what to do with one's life is left to society. This may be done cheerfully, and it may result in an apparently normal and wholesome life. As an act of self-abandonment and of acquiescence in estrangement, however, it can come only out of despair.

Every movement in the direction of community, then, occasions personal vulnerability, and every device for eliminating this vulnerability amounts to a refusal, through pride or self-abandonment, of finite and erring selfhood. Clearly entry into community is unnatural and difficult. The most serious and widespread fault in the existing literature on community is an unrealistic optimism. Entry into community is assumed on all sides to be readily accomplished and altogether agreeable. Even Martin Buber, probably the greatest philosopher of community in our time, is insensitive to the risks inherent in address and attention. If such optimism were well founded, however, the tragic character of human history would be inexplicable. How could we account for the indifference, fear, and hatred that repeatedly separate individuals, groups, and nations? Communication indeed is simple and at last fulfilling. But it is desperately hard. This should not surprise us, for it accords with the ancient wisdom that things of supreme worth are not achieved without suffering and purification.

Groundlessness and Pride

We now encounter a question that may sound strange but is unavoidable and deeply divides philosophers and nations. This is whether man can establish his own ground. If he can, it is not faith that is needed for overcoming shame and entering into community, but rather action. If he cannot, however, then groundlessness is a religious situation.

The reason this question may sound strange is partly that I have assumed groundlessness to be a real state of being, not an illusion. I have assumed that recent phenomenology, which depicts human existence as characterized by qualities such as factuality and indeterminacy, is accurate. Nevertheless, groundlessness might characterize human existence actually but not essentially. Groundlessness might be accidental; it might, for example, be an aspect of man's historical situation, and it might, accordingly, be a condition that man could remove by reconstituting that situation.

There are great thinkers who have implicitly attributed to man the power of overcoming groundlessness. Nietzsche and Marx, for example, called in effect for human self-grounding. For Nietzsche, this was a demand upon personal freedom and power; the Superman was envisioned as possessing a splendor that provided—first of all, for himself, but indirectly for all—a reason for being, a human identity, moral justification. For Marx, human self-grounding was a problem of social reconstruction. Groundlessness was not an ontological state, but a result of particular and temporary social derangements; overcoming these derangements through communism would mean the recovery of human command over the ground of existence. A member of the ideal society that Marx envisioned would, no more than Nietzsche's Superman, be afflicted with a sense of arbitrary, unsettled, and unacceptable selfhood. Both Nietzsche and Marx fulfilled Dostoevsky's prophecy that human beings would repudiate the God-man, Christ, and would exalt in his place the man-god. In the thought of Nietzsche, the man-god was an individual splendid in power and solitude; in the thought of Marx, a being of perfect communality. In both cases, although in different ways, man was to be his own creator and redeemer.

The visions of Nietzsche and Marx are of an apocalyptic—and for many people correspondingly implausible—character. But the far more prosaic outlook of many sober middle-class people in the Western nations also embodies a great deal of confidence in man's capacity to establish his own ground. This capacity is expected to manifest itself, not in the appearance of unprecedented human greatness or in revolutionary action, but rather in the advance of science and technology. Scientific understanding is expected to encompass not only the physical universe but human nature and society, and in consequence man is expected to gain the power of controlling for his own benefit all of reality, including his own psyche and the societies he constructs.

How valid is confidence of this kind? To me it seems that although the question of whether man possesses a power of self-grounding is not logically absurd, once that question has been explicitly articulated, it can be answered in one way alone. Man cannot establish his own ground because he is finite and mortal and because he is morally flawed. For such intoxicating prophecies as those of Nietzsche and Marx, or even the expectations of many believers in science and technology, to be fulfilled, man would have to conquer his finitude and overcome death. He would have to understand and command all of being, thus attaining complete transcendence—a state beyond history, time, and objective reality. And he would have to occupy this exalted state in wisdom and love. Otherwise, the only change in his existence would be that he himself would be the author of his arbitrary and unacceptable being. Groundlessness would inhere in a malign omnipotence.

Death is a particularly telling demonstration of our groundlessness. Neither Nietzsche nor Marx faced the fact that human beings will always, even in the most advanced stages of history, have to die. Neither took into account our invincible ignorance concerning death—that we will never know, with the certainty of experience and awareness, what death means. To look on death as a mere natural fact, like the process of digestion, is a comforting illusion. It is rather a boundary-line drawn around the world of natural facts. It marks out unmistakable limits upon human power and understanding.

As for our moral flaws, it may simply be noted how questionable it is to suppose that one who finds himself morally unacceptable can by his own efforts surmount that condition. By what powers that are not themselves morally perverted might this be done? It is of course often denied that our consciousness of moral unacceptability is veridical. But, as exemplified in the tyrannies to which Marxism has given rise, these denials are rarely if ever confirmed by their consequences. On the contrary, it is apparently through being defiantly oblivious to our morally flawed condition that we allow it to congeal in the form of actual misdeeds. In Christian terms, through pride we make the state of original sin (moral groundlessness) manifest in particular sins.

This rule may be applied to the state of groundlessness as a whole. Although we cannot establish our own ground, we persistently try to do so and we persistently fall under the illusion that we have succeeded. We rarely achieve lucidity concerning our ontological and moral state. In thus forgetting our limits we unwittingly conspire with finitude and mortality and we abet our perversities. In our self-induced blindness, we encounter our limits in more shocking and disastrous ways and indulge the evil in our nature more unrestrainedly than we otherwise would. Some of this is expressed in the Greek idea of hubris and of the nemesis that it was apt to call forth. Also, through efforts at self-grounding, we conspire with finitude and mortality and with our own destructive impulses by cutting ourselves off from any ground beyond ourselves. We render our limits absolutely conclusive—which is what Paul may have had in mind when he said that the sting of death is sin. We do not in these ways create our groundlessness, but we do accept and confirm it.

All of this has an important bearing on the problem of interpreting shame. If groundlessness is a manifestation of man's ontological and moral state, then shame is veridical. It is an impassioned realization of the human situation, insofar as that situation is disclosed in experience and awareness.

Many writers and thinkers have tried to avoid drawing conclusions of this sort by invoking great men. Rather than appealing beyond man altogether, they have appealed beyond the average man. Thus Nietzsche tried to overcome his despair and hatred of human beings as he saw them in his time by looking ahead to the godlike beings that a few were to become. All of us, I think, respond to visions such as Nietzsche's. A few, scattered through the ages, confront their groundlessness with impressive dignity and imagination, and from figures like Michelangelo and Beethoven we derive prophetic hope. But even the few fall strikingly short of perfection. This is perhaps most definitively manifest in the enduring distinction between the saint and the genius—between those who are very good in themselves but create little or nothing, and those who create works of great splendor but in themselves are not very good. That such supreme creative figures as Michelangelo and Beethoven were so unmistakably human and not divine tells us a great deal about man in his worldly essence. Moreover, whatever heights have been reached by a few, we are surely not justified in ignoring all others in forming our estimates of man and his possibilities. The mediocrity of most people and the degradation of some testify no less compellingly than the greatness of a few to man's fundamental condition and character.

Community, Faith, and Self

This line of thought brings us to a preliminary answer to the question posed at the beginning of this essay: is community a purely natural phenomenon? The answer is that shame, and hence the risk of address and attention, can be overcome only by a sense of self-respect, and that depends on faith.

It is plain why meeting the risks of communication depends on gaining respect for oneself. The dangers inherent in serious speaking and listening, where one hazards beliefs crucial to his own being and confesses his most disquieting doubts, can be rationally faced only by a person who is assured of his own worth. These dangers can be faced only by someone with enough self-respect not to be preoccupied with the possibility that his words will be rejected or misunderstood and not to be humiliated by the realization of having something to learn from others. Where self-respect is lacking, human relationships are apt to become testing grounds where insecure individuals try to convince themselves and others of their own worth. The quest for honor replaces the quest for truth; and community, as a consequence, is subverted.

The shame that arises from an impression of groundlessness is, broadly, an absence of self-respect. In the realization of factuality, one feels merely accidental; in the realization of indeterminacy, one's being appears to be arbitrarily chosen; in the realization of unacceptability, one has a sense of being unauthorized, subject to condemnation. It is when selfhood is experienced in these ways that address and attention become insupportable.

Since man cannot supply his own ground, however, he cannot at will overcome his factuality, indeterminacy, and unacceptability. This is why faith is necessary for community to be possible. Although man cannot create his own ground, he can affirm it in an act of free orientation toward transcendence, toward that which lies beyond the bounds of objectifying intelligence. Whether he is objectively correct in doing this cannot be determined or even, properly speaking, asked, since he is relating himself to nonobjective reality. In doing this, however, he recasts his own understanding of himself. He attributes to himself a reason for being, an identity, and a dignity that are not evident to observation.

This may seem to be a highly willful procedure, a matter of deliberately revising the disclosures of experience. Faith does not necessarily deny objective data, however, as we saw in Chapter II; it has to do with what lies beyond objective data. It arises, moreover, not as a human design, but only in response to what is understood as an act of divine revelation. Thus, for example, the major tenets of Christian faith are not viewed by any Christian as a human cultural creation; they are viewed as interpretations of divine acts.

Christianity illustrates not only the nonarbitrary character of faith, however, but also the role of faith in overcoming shame and opening the way to community. The doctrine of divine creation counters the impression of the mere factuality of one's being; the doctrine of redemption implies that man has a destiny, and this divests his indeterminacy (his freedom) of the gratuitousness that it seems to entail; the doctrine of forgiveness denies unacceptability.

The experience of shame, of the risks of communication, and of the consequent dependence of community on faith, however, is a disclosure of the ontological situation of every human being. Hence its implications reach further than we have so far recognized. They concern not only the self but others too.

Community, Faith, and Others

Community depends not only on respect for oneself, but on respect for others as well. Even if free of shame, we do not address or offer attention to those for whom we have no respect. No doubt there are many useful, admirable, and pleasant relationships that do not depend on respect. I may work with someone merely because he is at hand and is familiar with the job to be done; I may help someone in trouble because I am sorry for him; I may seek the companionship of someone because he is sympathetic or amusing. But when it comes to speaking of the things I greatly care about or of offering sustained attention of a kind in which my own being is thoroughly engaged, respect is absolutely indispensable.

Moreover, it seems worth noting—although the point is somewhat difficult—that respect for others is probably necessary indirectly if one is to gain respect for oneself. Selfhood does not take shape in isolation; one has a self to respect only so far as one has lived with and for other human beings. But one has done this only so far as one has had respect for them. In this sense, respect for others is prior to respect for oneself. No doubt the two kinds of respect are mutually supportive. But writers today so commonly emphasize the necessity of respecting oneself before offering oneself to others that it seems worth emphasizing the counter-necessity—that of respecting others before one is in any position to gain a self that can be offered to others. Seen from this point of view, the shame arising from groundlessness is overcome neither by winning the respect of others nor, where that is not accomplished, by a defiant affirmation of oneself. It is the affirmation of others that must come first of all.

Understanding the true breadth of the problem of respect, however, enables us to understand the true breadth of shame. Shame is an experience of one's own groundlessness. But it is at the same time an experience of the universal condition of man. In shame that is fully lucid, one perceives that every human being exists in a state of factuality, indeterminacy, and moral unacceptability. Hence, in a state of shame one does not face others who command respect; one discovers, when the full meaning of his state of mind is comprehended, that he is ashamed for all. And one does not overcome shame only by learning to respect himself; he must learn to respect everyone.

Shame, then, inhibits the communal impulse from both sides. In my awareness of my own groundlessness I recoil from communication. But if I gather myself together and engage in an act of address or attention in spite of my shame, then I am disappointed. I discover that those whom I address or to whom I attend are not better grounded—not more clearly conscious of their ultimate origins and ends, not more securely established in their own being, not possessed of greater moral self-assurance—than I am myself.

Only at this point in the dialectic of communication do I comprehend fully the nature of shame and the problem of respect. Both include all human beings. Both include the side of address and the side of attention alike. In the experience of shame I discover man—so far as he is disclosed in experience and awareness—as a creature who is inadequate to the demands of communication. Thus I discover the need for finding a way of respecting man, both myself and all others.

It must be understood that the issue of respect arises in relation to every human being I encounter, without exception. No human being is wholly without the capacity for objectifying another, hence no human being is so contemptible as not to be a possible agent of shame. Further, to discover that another human being is contemptible is always upsetting; if it seems otherwise, this is due to pride that is desperately in need of sustenance. The communal impulse is universal, and to encounter human beings who, like mere things in the world, are enclosed in their own being and unavailable for communication can never (apart from the effects of a desperate pride) be anything but disappointing and disturbing. We forget this only because it happens so frequently that we take it for granted. We are hardened to a world incongruous with our essential communal disposition.

Community, then, depends on conquering shame, and this comes about through a respect that comprises not only oneself but all other human beings. In addition to respect for persons, however, community depends on another kind of respect—that is, for truth.

That community depends on respect for truth is implied by the definition of community worked out in Chapter II—that community is inquiry. Community is a sharing of being, and since we do not dwell fully and steadily in the presence of being, community is a common search for being, a communicative effort to understand. If truth were worthless, serious communication would have no occasion or purpose. Human relationships would have no aim but cooperative action or mutual diversion.

Is truth worthless? It is strange that the question is so rarely asked, for the answer is not self-evident. It seems that the modern age has inherited from Greek antiquity and the Christian Middle ages a religious reverence for truth and that we have rather casually combined this reverence with pragmatic respect in the form of an assumption that truth is useful. Yet if we were to adhere to the logic of modern secularism, being would no longer seem to reflect the divine and truth would lose, in our eyes, all intrinsic value. And if we were to be more critical in our pragmatism, we would see that some truths, such as those concerning the ultimate fate of the earth and of human life upon it (not to speak of all those truths that are politically inconvenient), might be so unsettling that it would be better for them to remain unknown. In sum, setting aside faith in God, no reason remains for assuming that truth must be sought or that inquiring communication is a noble activity. The ideal of community is undermined.

It is possible to introduce this issue somewhat incidentally and to treat it briefly because, important as it is, it is an aspect of the issue of respect for persons. Truth in a comprehensive sense concerns humanity —the situation of human beings in the universe, and their ultimate prospects. Respect for truth is bound to be proportional to respect for persons.

If human beings in the context of the most comprehensive understanding are seen to be groundless—each one accidental, indeterminate, unacceptable—then the truth must be distressing and even debilitating. It would be difficult to make a strong case for our revering it or searching persistently for it. Certain limited truths, such as those of mathematics, might be intrinsically valuable on account of their beauty; others might be useful. But the truth in its entirety might better remain undiscovered. In this irreligious age we tend to forget that truth has been revered, as can be seen in the thought of Plato and Aristotle, of the Stoics, of Augustine, because it concerns the ground of humanity. But if no such ground exists, then truth can only show us an abyss of which we might better remain in ignorance.

On the other hand, if human groundlessness is only an impression conveyed by experience and awareness, if a full and integrated consciousness will show each human being as the possessor of a destiny—a reason for being, a determinate identity, an ultimate justification— arising from the ground of being, then discovery of the full truth is suitably the supreme purpose of human life. To know the truth is in this case to enter into conscious and responsible relationships with the ground of being. Communication, as the common search for truth, becomes the decisive expression of love.

Augustine asserted that we must have faith in order to attain understanding. The idea to which these reflections have brought us is very close to this: that we must have faith in order to inquire, that is, to pursue understanding in common, to engage in communication of utmost seriousness.

Some may feel, however, that this conclusion depends on an exaggerated pessimism. Do not human beings simply as we observe them command some respect? Does not the truth as brought out by scientists, historians, and others have a charm and usefulness that is independent of faith? In order to answer these questions it is necessary to mark out more carefully the position we have reached.

Natural Respect and Transcendental Respect

There seems to me little question that a degree of respect for human beings as well as for truth is a natural possibility. Some theologians, of whom Karl Barth is the most eminent contemporary example, assert the total depravity of man, thus implying that no person alone, apart from God's grace, deserves respect. Nevertheless, we all encounter persons whom we spontaneously respect. Some may be famous figures in cultural and political life, some may be friends or acquaintances. Moreover, we can all find in practically everyone particular characteristics that call for respect. If we consult our daily experiences and our spontaneous reactions, we may discover that there is not a single person to whom the principle of total depravity applies.

We are told by theologians such as Barth that the natural qualities we respect have their ultimate source in God, and this may be so. But what matters in the issue immediately before us is that these qualities are present in natural man and are apparent to natural intelligence. One is not compelled by the inadequacy of nature to fall back on faith—at least not for granting human beings a limited measure of respect.

As for truth, here too a measure of natural respect is possible. Even if human life is groundless, there still are realms of order and beauty that command attention for their own qualities. No appeal to faith is needed to justify our studying them. This is not to speak of the fact that truth may be prized also for its utility, although devotion to comprehensive and ultimate truth cannot thus be justified.

Does this imply that community is, as modern man avers, a natural phenomenon and independent of faith? Undoubtedly, just as a degree of natural respect for human beings and for truth is possible, so is a degree of natural community. Men as natural beings, men without faith, can at least within limits enter into authentic communication.

Everything depends, however, on what the limits of natural community are. We must ask whether the measure of community that natural respect makes possible corresponds with the measure of community that man in his communal essence necessarily seeks. If it does not, then the argument points toward a very different resolution of the issue than the possibility of natural community may at first suggest.

Many people today feel that it is anachronistic and unworthy of an enlightened age to speak of finitude and sin. But in discounting these overwhelming realities we have acquiesced in a sentimental and befuddled appraisal of man; and we have done this while supposedly divesting ourselves of superstition. The typical enlightened person of the present day has rejected Christianity and yet has retained the Christian notion that every person manifests a singular and inexpressible worth. This has come to be referred to as a person's "dignity" or "infinite value." But inquiry is seldom made as to the source or nature of this quality or of our consciousness of it. It is casually assumed that the dignity of the individual is a natural endowment and is apparent to natural reason. But it was not apparent to the natural reason of the greatest of the pagans. Plato did not discern an indefeasible dignity in every individual, and Aristotle did not consider every human being as possessed of infinite value. Both thinkers accepted slavery. Both prescribed exclusive culture and aristocratic government.

The truth is that human beings, as disclosed to observation and reason, are of limited value—finite, mortal, and morally imperfect. Some surpass others in such qualities as courage and intelligence, but none possess these qualities without limits of degree and time. So long as no appeal is made to faith, our respect for human beings must be proportioned to these limits. For some we may have great respect, but for others we can have very little. To none—so long as we adhere to the judgments of natural reason—can we assign infinite value.

The consequence is that we cannot *reasonably* will communities that are not severely limited. We cannot reasonably will that all men should come together without distinctions, such as those based on education and demonstrated ability. We cannot reasonably will the abolition of arrangements that permit individuals to withdraw as often and as completely as they choose from human society. We cannot reasonably will societies without hierarchies of power. It may seem that all of this is not so bad, that we can still seek out and live in the company of the few individuals who deserve respect. There is still friendship and marriage.

Certainly limited communities are better than nothing—so much better that they can keep one from despair. When surrounded by disintegration and hatred, however, they are far more fragile and less fulfilling than is generally realized. Several great novels have shown the inescapably tragic character of personal relations where encompassing relations are seriously disturbed; examples are Boris Pasternak's *Doctor Zhivago* and Malcolm Lowry's *Under the Volcano*. Deep personal relations can never be a refuge from historical disorder but only a place where the anguish of such disorder is fully experienced. The reason for this is not only that immediate relationships are inevitably affected by surrounding social conditions (Zhivago and Lara, for example, are physically torn apart by the Russian Revolution). It is also that we cannot be satisfied with exclusive relationships. Contrary to the myth of romantic love and to common bourgeois sentiments concerning the family, man is a cosmopolitan being. This is uncompromisingly affirmed at the summits of moral thought—by Isaiah, by the Stoics, by Kant.

Hence nothing can keep us from looking with communal hopes and aspirations to the encompassing world. When we do so, however, these hopes and aspirations are painfully checked. The community we long for is wide enough to embrace men of all civilizations, even the most backward and repellant; egalitarian enough to take no notice of differences in intelligence, education, or moral worth; tolerant enough to provide a hearing even for doctrines that are apparently perverse and erroneous; merciful enough to open its doors and accord opportunities of reform to every criminal. But community of this kind requires a respect for persons that is not justified by their natural character. As a nisus toward human beings, love is universal and indiscriminate. As a rational policy it is exclusive, hierarchical, and judgmental. A communal aristocracy like that outlined by Plato or suggested in notes by Nietzsche is probably the highest ideal that can be reached apart from faith.[3] Potentially communal institutions, such as tolerance, majority rule, and equal rights, are by no means unchallengeable on the grounds of expediential calculation to which natural intelligence is confined. In practice they often prove inconvenient or worse, and then are seen to depend on a respect for every person—a refusal to measure human worth—that cannot be justified by observation or reason.

3. See particularly Nietzsche's *The Will to Power*, trans. Walter Kaufmann and R. J. Hollingdale (New York: Random House, 1967).

The community to which we aspire is correspondingly limitless in relation to the truth. We do not seek to share just some things, but all things; this is shown by the boundless range of literary art. The communal impulse is not confined to objects of experience but pertains to every mode of consciousness; this is demonstrated in the history of religion.

It may thus be said that natural respect is not enough; community depends on transcendental respect. This is accorded when respect is called forth by something beyond the natural characteristics of its object. When a human being disgusting in personal appearance, ruined in moral character, and incapable of performing any useful social function is nevertheless an object of serious attention—which occasionally happens in the welfare and criminal processes of modern nations—he is accorded transcendental respect. If the quality that calls forth transcendental respect is to be defined, it may be said to be a quality of infinity. We express this when we speak of "the infinite value of the individual." Not, of course, that finitude is no longer regarded as real and important. One who commands transcendental respect, however, like the "Thou" of Martin Buber, "fills the sky." He is not reducible to the limitations disclosed in experience and defined through objective appraisal. Therefore, although he is finite, he is not *merely* finite, and although he is sinful in pride and self-abandonment, he is not comprehensible wholly in terms of the character he thus creates. There is a quality in him by virtue of which he transcends his finitude and his faults. Transcendental respect arises when one senses that all limitations, both those suffered and those chosen, are inconclusive.

Through transcendental respect we are freed from the limits and hierarchies dictated by observation and reason. We rise above shame without resorting to pride. Both I myself and those I encounter are placed on a plane of communal opportunity.

It is often argued by those unwilling to appeal to faith that rationality itself entails an imperative of universal communication. It is held that to reason exhaustively is to listen to all, to open the reasoning process to everyone. This view is implicit in the thought of John Stuart Mill, and it has an important place in the writings of Jürgen Habermas. It is essentially a claim that anything less than universality presupposes dogmatism, an arbitrary exclusiveness in the comradeship of reason.

This answers, implicitly, a question raised at the outset of these reflections as to whether there can be such a thing as tacit faith. It was suggested in connection with this question that the spiritual relationships—the relationships of man and transcendence—actually prevailing at any particular time may be quite different from the social relationships comprised in religious institutions. It was suggested that the actual spiritual situation may not be accurately reflected even in the conscious convictions of individuals. Seeing the incongruity between our communal aspirations and manifest worldly realities, and seeing also the communal openness and courage of many without faith of the kind expressed in institutional or creedal commitments, it is difficult to deny the reality of tacit faith. "I girded thee," says God in the Book of Isaiah, "though thou has not known me."[4]

Many people today, of course, find all concepts of transcendence implausible and unappealing. This is probably due to various conditions, but perhaps above all to the spectacular achievements of science and technology. If, without faith, we can do things as dramatic as releasing nuclear energy and exploring space, then surely, without faith, we can do something as simple and inconspicuous as entering into community. But the preceding discussion suggests that community is a greater and rarer achievement than we think. Our experience in the twentieth century suggests this too. Among all of our triumphs, one small problem—community—has remained unsolved, and that single failure threatens to undo all else that we have accomplished.

Faith and Hope

With our attention thus turned toward the future, we can see that transcendental respect places very different prospects before us than does natural respect. If we confine ourselves to natural respect, we say in effect that there are no prospects ever of fulfilling man's impulse toward community. We do this in two ways.

First, we imply that there is no force in the universe making for community except that constituted by our own communal powers. These are slight. The finitude and moral imperfection that place limits on man's claims to respect place limits also on his powers of granting respect. Even if there were some sense in saying that each person in his

4. Isaiah 45:5

natural state of being is of infinite value, we could not reasonably expect natural man to possess or to act upon this knowledge. Our capacities for discerning dignity and according respect are feeble. Sin is essentially a withholding of respect where it is due, in pride through exclusive self-assertion, in self-abandonment through acquiescing in a general state of human objectification such as that brought about by tyranny. Consequently, even where human beings deserve respect, often they do not receive it. Every crime, such as robbery or murder, expresses radical disrespect. Also, the subtle indifference and disdain that pervade personal relations without ever taking the form of crime reveal an absence of respect. And human beings frequently fail to respect not only others but themselves as well. This is evident in striking ways, as in suicide or extreme dissipation, and also in more or less normal patterns of behavior, as in lives of incessant busyness in which there is never time for leisured companionship.

A refusal of faith, which amounts to a refusal of transcendental respect, presupposes a universe in which all hope of community depends on man himself. It also presupposes a universe structured in a way that is antithetical to community. This is the second way in which, by confining ourselves to natural respect, we say that there are no prospects ever of fulfilling the communal impulse.

The natural conditions hedging about the possibilities of community conditions revealed in experience—are elemental: distance in space, separation in time, death, ignorance. One can gain full relationships at best with only a few of the myriad persons living and dead. Numberless multitudes have died before one was born and will be born after one has died, and almost all of these are for all time out of reach. The personal relationships we do achieve are certain to be destroyed sooner or later by death; and absolutely every act of communication is disfigured by the limits and errors of our knowledge. These conditions are so all-pervasive that we seldom think of them in connection with community. It is plain, however, that they entail insuperable estrangement. Communal relationships are possible, but they are pathetically frail and small. Not only are they under sentence of the death that each participant must suffer; they are surrounded and nearly overwhelmed by vast planetary spaces and endless historical ages.

The faith that underlies transcendental respect places one in a very different universe, one in which the dominant mood of a communal relationship can be hope rather than tragedy. From the standpoint of observation and reason, a communal relationship is a mirror of human finitude and imperfection and also of an impersonal and indifferent universe. It is a poignant reminder of death, of purposeless history, of silent space. From the standpoint of faith, however, an act of communication shows forth images of a very different kind. Attention and address become intimations of the final subordination of the world to community, of worldly calculation to respect. They become eschatological occurrences.

Christianity is the archetypal religion not only of transcendental respect but also of community. This is sometimes obscured by the symbol of the crucifixion. Jesus was abandoned by all others and killed. Hence he seems to represent complete alienation, an individual alone and in opposition to society. It is true that Jesus was in opposition to society. But he was not in opposition to community. He embodied ultimate truth and limitless love and thus is always said to represent the appearance in the world not just of an individual but of a kingdom—the kingdom of God. Christianity, then, discloses the fate of community within the world—the universe presupposed by natural respect. Christianity also, however, discloses the inconclusiveness of this fate. One may see in the resurrection a symbol of the ultimate communality of the universe.

Some readers may feel that even if these reflections are sound, faith still leads with logical inevitability to intolerance and repression. If so, faith is fundamentally antithetical to community, in spite of all that has been said, for community depends on freedom. A sense that faith and freedom are antithetical seems deeply rooted in the modern mind, a residue perhaps of the experience of religious intolerance and conflict that inaugurated the modern era. Whether they are is an important question. In bringing this essay to a close, we must examine it.

Faith and Freedom

The novels of Dostoevsky contain a powerful argument to the effect that it is the absence of faith, not faith itself, that jeopardizes freedom. If there is no God, Dostoevsky believed, it follows that "all is permitted."

Respect for life and freedom fades. The murderer and the tyrant become ideal human types. Dostoevsky's reasons for believing this probably lay not in the primitive notion that a valid moral law presupposes a legislator and enforcer, but in views similar to those developed in the course of these reflections. To begin with, he was apparently convinced that the idea of human dignity was implicitly religious and that atheism was therefore subversive of social unity and civilized government. He assigned particular importance to the idea of personal immortality. But he believed not only that atheism undermined respect for others; he saw it also as leading to gross and dangerous distortions of one's respect for himself. More precisely, he saw atheism as a source of overwhelming pride. Once God disappears from the horizon of the universe, man tries to become a god himself. The God-man gives way to the man-god. The implications of these two developments together—the collapse of respect for every man and the rise of self-deified humans—are tyrannical. Some of Dostoevsky's fascination today is owing to his prophetic anticipation of the subhuman malevolence and superhuman pretensions of twentieth-century tyrants.

Dostoevsky's views constitute a response to the objection that faith subverts freedom.[5] So far as those views are summed up in the statement that faith underlies respect and respect freedom, they are perhaps sufficiently explained and defended in the preceding pages. So far as Dostoevsky's views constitute a claim that faith bars tyrannical pride, however, further comment may be appropriate, for this is a matter we have considered only slightly. I shall not try to interpret Dostoevsky's conscious thoughts but only to elaborate upon his central idea.

That idea, as I understand it, is humility. "God is in heaven," says Ecclesiastes, "and thou upon earth."[6] Faith in God requires conscious and unqualified recognition of the mere humanity of man. God is denied if man thinks that he himself is God. Faith exalts man, it is true, but only on the grounds of his connection with God. It assigns him only a

5. There is no good book-length study of Dostoevsky's political ideas, so far as I am aware, and partly for this reason the notion that in his politics Dostoevsky was nothing but a theocratic reactionary continues to prevail. Perhaps the best book for correcting this misconception is Nicolas Berdyaev's *Dostoevsky*, trans. Donald Attwater (New York: World Publishing Co., 1957).

6. Ecclesiastes 5:2

limited value in his separate selfhood, and it unqualifiedly condemns any philosophy or movement that grants absolute value to a human faculty or a human institution.

Thus, for example, faith requires that we acknowledge the finitude and fallibility of the intellect. It presupposes intellectual uncertainty and condemns any claim, like that often associated with Marxism, that the complete and final truth has been scientifically understood. The implications of this view are libertarian. The intellect is never warranted in being dictatorial. In its true nature it is a faculty of inquiry. This applies to truth of any kind, but it applies with particular force to the truth comprised in faith. Nicolas Berdyaev argues that man's relations with God are not subject even to the kind of coercion exercised by the intellect, the coercion inherent in evidence and in logic.[7]

Faith, then, requires intellectual humility. It also requires social and political humility. The tendency of many people to make a god of society, a tendency that is fully developed in the sociology of Emile Durkheim, is an enormity from the standpoint of faith. It hardly needs to be added that making a god of some human being, such as Stalin or Hitler, is a like enormity. What does seem worthy of emphasis, however, is the secularism inherent in this view. If God dwells in heaven and not on earth, He does not inhabit any order that we human beings build on earth. Only by insisting on the earthly character of society, on the finitude and fallibility of every human order, do we keep ourselves in a position in which we can recognize a Being who is falsified and implicitly denied if treated as a being within the world.

Dictatorial faith, then, is self-contradictory. Man may become sure of God, but not of the proper ways of speaking about and worshipping God. Those who claim the latter assurance refuse, in effect, to remain on earth where they belong. It can be argued that they are implicitly atheistic even when they are formally religious. This implies that certain attitudes toward the churches, not only on the part of Catholics but on the part of Protestants as well, have amounted to an idolatrous perversion of faith. Paul indicated how we should look upon the doctrines and institutions in which faith is embodied when he wrote that "we have

---

7. See, for example, Nicolas Berdyaev, *Truth and Revelation*, trans. R. M. French (New York: Collier Books, 1953).

this treasure in earthen vessels, that the excellency of the power may be of God, and not of us."[8]

Has not Christianity, however, always claimed to be the one and only truth? How can that claim be anything in the field of politics if it is not dictatorial and totalitarian? Such an objection may seem quite compelling if Christianity is seen as one doctrine among other doctrines, with Christians differing from non-Christians primarily in believing that their own doctrine is the only one that is true. The Gospels, however, do not present a doctrine; they present a story. Christ did not claim to know or to state the truth, but to *be* the truth; and as sweeping as that claim may be, it is essentially tolerant, for a truth inseparable from the being of a particular person is not the sort of truth one can be forced to accept. Furthermore, the earliest Christian theology did not assert that the Christian outlook should be accepted and every other outlook rejected. It asserted that Christ was the Logos, and it thus implied that Christ is a truth that might be found in some measure in every outlook—a sun of being, in Plato's metaphor—and manifest wherever there is light.

It is possible to construe Christianity as a bestowal of liberty—not of truth, but of liberty to search for truth. As Dostoevsky brings out in "The Legend of the Grand Inquisitor," Christ did not come down from the cross, did not turn the stones into bread, did not claim worldly authority. He did not provide us with the certainty to be derived from miracles; he did not help to meet our physical needs; and he did not contribute to the psychological security we would have found had he taken on supreme worldly authority. By doing none of these things, he made Christianity enigmatic and questionable and, in consequence, an almost overwhelming demand on human freedom. Franz Kafka once remarked, apropos of Christianity, "What a cruel God it is who makes it possible for his creatures not to recognize him."[9] A Christian might answer that such cruelty is only God's willingness to leave us free.

We noted near the outset of these reflections Feuerbach's view that we attribute our own best qualities to God, thus alienating our human

8. II Corinthians 4:7
9. Gustav Janouch, *Conversations with Kafka*, trans. Goronwy Rees (2nd ed.; New York: New Directions Books, 1971), 116.

grandeur. Considering the age-long tendency to envision God as a despot, taking offense at every departure from doctrines never made entirely clear, we might better say that it is our *worst* qualities that we attribute to God. Rather than alienating our grandeur, we try to shed responsibility for our pettiness and pride. Believers and atheists are generally at one in doing this, although atheists may remain nearer the truth, for they reject so degraded a god.

The whole argument of this essay suggests that we should question the effort to conceive of God in terms of power. What can a God who is primarily power have to do with community? Of course every conception of God's being and presence is inadequate. But rather than thinking of God as a power producing observable results, perhaps we should think of Him as a source of freedom and mutual understanding. He might be more safely defined not as power, but, following the First Epistle of John, as love.

IX / TRANSCENDING TRAGEDY: THE IDEA OF CIVILITY

The Individual and History

In concluding, we shall give our attention to the two polar realities with which we have been concerned throughout these reflections: the individual and history.

We are concerned with the individual because it is the individual, stripped of communal relationships, that our realization of the tragic character of the communal ideal leaves standing before us. We are bound to ask what the ideal of community can mean to one whose fate is estrangement. The twentieth century has become intensely conscious of the human being in his singularity, alienated from society and history, abandoned to a state of isolation and defenselessness. Migrant workers and displaced persons starkly exemplify this state in the world around us; Zhivago and Meursault (Camus' "Stranger") exemplify it in fiction. If these reflections have not misled us, however, contemporary alienation has made us conscious, not of a peculiar and distinguishing experience (except possibly in intensity), but of the human state. Man is a communal being who, in his finitude, mortality, and pride, enters only fragmentary and ephemeral communities. What, then, can the ideal of community mean? Does it only remind us of all that we are inevitably denied?

We are concerned with history because, as we have already seen, when the communal ideal is fully unfolded, it is an ideal of oneness with history. The individual's communality is unbounded, and history is simply all humanity as seen in its temporal dispersion. Often alienation is experienced as historical alienation—the consciousness of being threatened and overwhelmed by the tide of world events. This consciousness was given classical expression in Tolstoy's *War and Peace*. Of course, a person could hardly gain oneness with history without entering into lesser associations. But the limitless character of human communality means that for fully lucid human beings, lesser associations mediate relationships with history.

It may help in focusing on man's concern with history to speak of *historicity*—a term somewhat bizarre in appearance, yet sharp and convenient.[1] Historicity belongs to anything that exists in history and is formed by history. We refer to the historicity of man when we say that not only his situation but his being itself is historical. We may also, however, refer to the historicity of entities other than man. All artifacts exist in history and are formed by history, and the same is true, in limits, of many animals, such as domesticated dogs and war-horses. Thus we may speak of the historicity both of Alexander the Great and of Bucephalus. But this brings before us a distinction that is important for understanding man's relationship with history. While Bucephalus *had a part* in history, we cannot say of the horse, as we can of Alexander, that it *participated* in history. To participate is to have a part consciously and deliberately—to *take* part. Participation in history may be defined as conscious and deliberate historicity. It means living one's destiny in a way that cannot be done by an animal but only by a human being. And it means living a destiny that is uniquely human, in that only man has a history.

At stake, then, are both one's connections with others and one's selfhood. If one could perfectly realize his historicity, the impulse toward community would be fulfilled. He would enter into a state of unity with all humanity and all times. Simultaneously he would become conscious of and responsibly live his own historical existence. Inhabiting all ages, he would, paradoxically, realize his innermost personal being. In sum, trying to take part in history is a search both for community and for selfhood.

The relative priority of these two aims—community and selfhood —is commonly misunderstood, however. As a result the participa-

---

1. Jaspers has devoted considerable attention to something he calls "historicity." See his *Philosophy*, trans. E. B. Ashton (Chicago: University of Chicago Press, 1970), II, 104–129. Jaspers uses the term very broadly, so that it usually seems to denote man's embeddedness not merely in historical events, properly speaking, but in any particular and unrepeatable set of circumstances.

tory relationship of man and history is obscured. Two misunderstandings are especially prevalent, one bearing on the importance, the other on the manner, of historical participation. These are serious enough to warrant brief examination.

Identity and Recognition

The first of these misunderstandings is inherent in the popular notion that only after "finding out who you are" can good relationships with others be established. Personal identity is prior to community.[2] Although exponents of this view often are self-consciously progressive in their attitudes, on this particular point they represent an old-fashioned individualism. They assume that individuals are substantially complete apart from society, that one may gain various satisfactions and benefits from society but not personal identity itself.

Such individualism is dubious. Doubt is cast on it by some of the greatest names and most powerful movements in modern social and political thought—by Hegel and idealism, by Marx and various types of radicalism, by Burke and the kind of conservatism associated with his name, and finally by Martin Buber and the existentialism that argues the possibility of "intersubjectivity." Doubt that personal identity exists prior to community arises also from a common personal experience: that everything a person does to define his own being—talking, listening, creating, following a vocation, and so forth—amounts to some kind of relationship or set of relationships. Pointing to the same conclusion is the simple fact that we can identify another person only in terms of relationships, such as occupation, status, and residence. To be, it seems, is to be related, and to be a certain person is to be situated in a certain way within a network of relationships.

This bears on our understanding of historical participation. If you already "know who you are," then taking part in history is perhaps desirable but it is not indispensible. If a person's identity derives from his relationships, however, then taking part in history has greater urgency. As a conscious and deliberate relationship with all who live and have ever lived, its value lies in the discovery of an identity in no way truncated or prematurely defined. The concept of responsible his-

---

2. For an intelligent expression of this view, see R. D. Laing, *The Divided Self: An Existential Study in Sanity and Madness* (Baltimore: Penguin Books, 1965).

toricity, incorporating the two aims of community and selfhood, indicates the true relationship of these aims: community—in the fullest sense, responsible historicity—is the matrix of selfhood.

A reader is bound to wonder, in the course of this discussion, how it is possible even to approach a state of relatedness as comprehensive as all of history. To answer this question fully will be to unfold the meaning of a concept briefly defined at the outset of these reflections—the concept of civility. Before that can be done, we must reflect on a second common misunderstanding concerning selfhood and community. This is the notion that what one needs from others is mainly to be "recognized."

Only by being recognized, it is said, can a person lay sure hold of his selfhood. Recognition is thus the supreme purpose with which one enters into human relationships. This misunderstanding is allied with the one just discussed in that the very use of the term *recognition* implies that personal identity precedes and is established independently of the relationship that comes into being in the act of recognition. Having criticized the idea that selfhood is prior to community, we are bound to question the common conception of recognition.

A sign that something is amiss may be seen in the fact that emphasizing recognition leads naturally, if not inevitably, to the notion that historical participation consists in achieving renown, in being remembered by posterity. But that may not happen until one is dead. Of what use is it then? And is it certain that posterity is just—that those who are remembered are remembered accurately and are precisely those who deserve to be remembered? And since posterity can remember only a handful from each generation, how can the vast multitudes destined for oblivion hope for selfhood? Questions of this sort impel us to ask whether it is true that being recognized is indispensable to one's humanity.

There are reasons for thinking that it is not. The most compelling of these reasons perhaps is found in the two principal archetypes of human excellence in Western culture—Socrates and Jesus. Each one of course finally was recognized, but only after suffering a humiliating and solitary death. Neither, while living, received recognition in which there was very much truth, and leaving no written testimony neither could have relied for recognition on posterity. Observations such as these, however, may only obscure what is most important, which is that neither one manifested much concern with being recognized. Their concern was not with anything they could receive but with the things they gave. What distinguishes them, as we look back, is their recognition of others—on the part of Socrates through unreserved availability for philosophical discourse, on the part of Jesus through a sacrificial life and death. No doubt it is burdensome and discouraging to be unrecognized. To hold that it is inevitably destructive of personal identity, however, is to invert the wisdom symbolized by Socrates and Jesus: that according, not receiving, recognition is what matters.

Common sense, moreover, seems to coincide with this wisdom. It is commonly held that those who pursue creative work, particularly in the arts, must often endure prolonged obscurity. The denial of recognition is thought of as a kind of furnace in which the selfhood of the creative person is forged. Such an image may be trite, but it would be difficult to claim that it is altogether untrue.

It is noteworthy that even Hegel, whose famous "lordship and bondage" section in *The Phenomenology of Mind* is a major source of the doctrine that what man needs from others is mainly recognition, seems finally to adopt a different view.[3] The struggle leading to the differentiation of lord and bondsman is a struggle for recognition; it is in this way that Hegel seems to point to recognition as the central issue of social life. Both sides fail, the lord because in enslaving his opponent he deprives him of his capacity for according valid recognition, the bondsman because he loses the struggle. The bondsman, however, is the one who is immediately and unmistakably denied recognition, and the bondsman is the one who is destined to make inward progress and to lead mankind out of the cul-de-sac of slavery. The destiny of the bondsman is not determined by some dialectical reversal through which recognition finally is gained, however. Rather, Hegel seems to say, it is determined by the suffering inherent in his bondage. Humanity arises from the very opposite of recognition, from obscurity—a point explosively restated by Marx.

We shall assume, then, that what is morally decisive is, rather than being recognized, the act of granting recognition. Proceeding on this

3. See Georg Wilhelm Friedrich Hegel, *The Phenomenology of Mind*, trans. J. Baillie (2nd ed.; New York: Macmillan & Co., 1931), 228–240.

assumption, the idea of participating in history comes more clearly into view. It may be understood as comprehensive recognition. One realizes his own historicity in recognizing the historicity of others—their freedom, their finitude, their temporality, and the conditions and events that have formed their lives.

The reason why man must try to do this also comes more clearly into view when recognizing others, rather than being recognized, is stressed. It becomes possible to see participation in history as an extension of personal love. Any such connection is ruled out by the prevailing idea, for loving means giving, whereas being recognized means receiving. It is difficult to construe the search for recognition as having anything to do with love. Not so the granting of recognition, for it may be said that this is what love is. A beloved friend or mate is one who is recognized steadily and truly. When one moves beyond immediate relationships into history, so long as one is trying to see and to appreciate people in their full reality—their historical reality— it may be said that the underlying principle remains the same, that of love.

This is not to suggest that there is any substitute for recognizing those encountered face-to-face. All of us have known people holding egregious political opinions who have nevertheless been warm and unselfish in their personal relations. All of us have probably sensed that the political opinions were somewhat redeemed by the personal relations, whereas, conversely, humane political opinions are apt to seem meaningless or hypocritical if accompanied by personal coldness or selfishness. Nevertheless, it is doubtful that our views of mankind at large are wholly without consequences for our personal relations. Hence there is a perilous incongruity in the posture of those who are historically irresponsible although personally humane. Personal love needs protection from the outworks built by responsible historicity, as the latter needs the authority and power that can be drawn from love. This mutually supportive relationship is possible only if we can assign moral priority to granting, rather than receiving, recognition.

To summarize, man enters into history for the sake both of relationships and of self-discovery. Only as a participant in the whole of history, not as a member of any lesser group, does he find his full, unrestricted humanity. The crucial act of participation is that of recognizing others, so far as possible all others, in their historicity. As already noted in Chapter VII, we can take part in history only fragmentarily and feebly. We can recognize only a few from all of the multitudes who have lived, and those uncertainly. The selfhood we reach in this way is correspondingly incomplete and obscure. Nonetheless, the standard of historical participation is not meaningless. Like the standard of love, it can guide us in forming our lives even though we can only begin to do all that it requires.

The problem before us, it may be well to recall, is that of how a solitary individual can affirm his communality in relation to history. I shall try to follow a clue to be found in *The Republic* at a point where Plato, in a mood of historical discouragement, notes that even if the philosopher cannot become a ruler of others he still can be a ruler of his own soul. From the apparent impossibility of a perfect historical polity, Plato thus appealed to the possibility of a perfect inner polity. Doing this, he envisioned a stance that is simultaneously solitary and communal. It is solitary in that it can be maintained by one person alone in a disintegrating world; it is communal in that it involves a responsible relationship between that one person and all other human beings.

This brings us back to an idea suggested at the outset of these reflections in response to the tragic character of community, which we are now in a position to explore more thoroughly.

The Idea of Civility

Before trying systematically to work out the idea of civility, it may be useful briefly to recall its general features. This can be done by noting the position into which an individual, adhering as fully as possible to the imperatives of his communal nature, is drawn by the communal disasters of our time.

One aspect of this position is historical detachment, standing off from events. In acknowledging the limits and unreliability of action, one is compelled to adopt, in some form and degree, a posture of inaction. This, as we shall see, does not mean completely withdrawing from political affairs, as prescribed by the Epicureans and the early Stoics. Programs may still be formulated and courses of action still pursued, but these must be tentative. Above all, one must not equate their fulfillment with personal salvation.

One must stand off from history in other ways as well. Giving up historical activism, one must also give up the ideological and group commitments entailed by that activism. Since community is not a historical possibility and cannot reasonably be an immediate object of action, no idea or system of ideas can either show forth the nature of earthly community or reliably prescribe ways of attaining it. All ideologies are more or less false. One ideology may be preferred to others, but this is legitimate only so far as the preferred ideology is a symbol rather than a concrete program—a symbol of intuitions and hopes that one does not try fully to translate into institutional or conceptual form. As for groups, a simple truth can be derived from our situation: that no group is a community and no group can create a community. Some groups are no doubt historically useful, but none deserve to be regarded in the way the working class and the Communist party have been regarded by many since the time of Marx. None show how man's communal destiny can be fulfilled. The same sort of thing must be said of leaders. One could hardly take part in historical life without adhering tentatively to certain leaders; but to think that any leader can create a community is to make a god out of a man.

Thus the foundering of our historical efforts forces us to place a certain distance—constituted of inaction, of doubt, and of limits on allegiance—between ourselves and history. Distance is not total separation, however. With regard to physical objects, the word *distance* designates a relationship, and so it is with regard to persons. One must stand off from history but not try to be wholly separate from history. The foregoing discussion indicates why not. In the first place, the immanence that bars man from controlling history as he desires also prevents him from wholly escaping history. Unavoidably each one is part of history, with not only the circumstances of his life but his very self historically formed. This is the meaning of historicity. To respond to the present communal impasse, as the Epicureans did to the downfall of the city-state, by prescribing total withdrawal would be delusory. If man could stand outside of history, he could stand above it and control it.

In the second place, total withdrawal is forbidden by our communal nature. We are bound to enter into relationships wherever we can, although these rarely constitute anything with the durability and fullness connoted by the word *community*. This is why we must try to understand and live our historicity even though we find that history is tragic.

In sum, communal disasters force us into a detachment that is a kind of relationship. We face the self-contradictory character of this position when we note a third aspect of it—that we must engage in action. We could not be responsibly related to others in a state of complete inaction. The circumstances requiring this conclusion arise from our situation, which checks not only heedless activism but heedless withdrawal as well. Even though community cannot be created through action, the absence of community necessitates action by giving rise to disorder. In a perfect community, all would come about through dialogue, but where community is lacking, order must be politically contrived.

If a person cannot completely give up action, neither can he completely divorce himself from ideologies and groups. Here also, *distance* becomes a term designating a relationship. When so many compromises have been accepted, however, does any coherent position remain?

Self-contradictory positions of a similar sort are not unheard of in our moral and religious traditions. Paul urges that "they that have wives be as though they had none; and they that weep, as though they wept not; and they that rejoice, as though they rejoiced not; and they that buy, as though they possessed not; and they that use this world, as not abusing it."[4] Our circumstances seemingly require that we act in a spirit of inaction—one of the main themes of the Bhagavad-Gita. It suggests the necessity of accepting an ideology while at the same time doubting it—something called for by so sane a thinker as John Locke.[5]

There is some authority, then, supporting the kind of moral equivocation seemingly forced upon us. On this basis, let us say that civility is the stance in which one lives and sustains the tensions experienced by a communal being in an anticommunal world. That may serve at any rate as a preliminary definition.

In proceeding to a more systematic definition, we must refrain from searching for precise rules. Readers may ask exactly what one must do, along the lines of voting, holding office, and so forth, in order to be

4. I Corinthians 7:29–31
5. See John Locke, *A Letter Concerning Toleration*, in *John Locke on Education and Politics*, ed. Howard R. Penniman (New York: D. Van Nostrand, 1947), 17–68. The idea that one should simultaneously believe and doubt is implicit in Locke's injunction to realize that you may be wrong.

civil. They may wonder at times whether civility comes down to anything more than regularly reading a good newspaper. Such questions are reasonable but cannot be answered here. This is not only because space is limited. Civility is necessitated by the very impossibility of subsuming man and history under rules. Consequently, it must be conceived of as creative. The only adequate definition of civility is one incarnate in the life of a civil person, a definition irreducible to detailed principles claiming universal validity.

Hence I shall try to formulate only a very general definition. The preceding discussion indicates the form that a definition of civility must assume, a form that reduces civility to three constituent elements.

1. HISTORICAL AUTONOMY. The primary question in every historical situation, for a civil person, is not "How can such and such a goal be reached?" but rather, "How should I bear myself?" With this query one recognizes what is within the scope of his responsibility. No one is responsible for achieving any particular historical result, but everyone is responsible for behaving in a certain manner. Giving primary consideration to one's personal bearing entails historical autonomy because it is an acceptance of personal responsibility and is consequently a refusal to vest in any human agency, or forsake for any ideology, one's powers of judgment and choice. Accordingly, one detaches himself from all absolute commitments and establishes the possibility that he will refuse a proposed action or break with a certain group or ideology. The inner statesmanship advocated by Plato was a kind of historical autonomy.

This does not spell indifference to historical results. Rather, it is a way of recognizing that the only significant results are those affecting the insights and passions of human beings. Significant historical changes, therefore, must occur within persons, and it follows that I am in a position to initiate historical change through the governance of my own soul. Doing this may be very little, measured against the vast scale of world history, but it is the little that I am clearly responsible for doing.

This attitude no doubt risks a kind of selfishness, that of caring for nothing but one's own rectitude. It does, however, meet two moral demands arising from the frustration of our communal hopes. One is that of acknowledging the objectification inherent in all political action. No government can devise political ends that benefit and command the voluntary allegiance of every member of a society. Hence to act politically is to use others as means; this is what creates the chasm between political action and community. While civility does not mean wholly abstaining from action, it does mean acting with an awareness that action is inherently depersonalizing and thus provides no direct access to the kind of unity that man seeks. It means, in this sense, acting with a bad conscience.

The second moral demand met by historical autonomy is that of giving up the pride expressed in striving for historical mastery. One grants the uncertainty of the future and concentrates, in pursuance of Plato's advice, on the politics of his own being. There would be pride, of course, in assuming that the self can be readily governed, even though history cannot. It belongs to man, however, to do all that he can to govern himself, whereas seeking to dominate history expresses cosmic presumption.

The refusal of pride is ordinarily a refusal of idolatry. There is perhaps a demonic pride that scorns allegiance to anything whatever beyond the self; the terrible figure of Stavrogin, in *The Possessed*, is a picture of such pride. But few have the strength for absolute self-assertion. Hence pride usually takes the form of reliance on something man has made, such as an institution or a system of thought. This is idolatry, and the idea that man can dominate history has generally taken the form of an idolatrous exaltation of a party or an ideology. In this light, civility becomes a rejection of finite gods, an insistence on holding oneself free for the totality of the human.

Historical autonomy must entail a readiness to disobey and resist. Some of the clearest examples of civility may be found among individuals, such as Thoreau, who are independent and courageous enough occasionally to rebel. Probably most of those who make up the immense law-abiding majority are not autonomous enough to be considered truly civil. Nevertheless, civility should not be equated with habitual resistance. There could be no order and no world in which civility is possible, unless everyone normally obeyed. A civil person must take this into account.

The second element in civility is the relationship implicit in distance.

2. COMPREHENSIVE COMMUNALITY. This is perhaps a barbarous phrase, but it accurately denotes a certain way of relating oneself to

mankind. To be comprehensively communal is, first of all, to be unreservedly attentive, not only to be attuned to man's voice wherever it can be heard, but to search out unvoiced experiences. Thus civility is manifest in Dr. Gachet's support for Cézanne and Van Gogh when they were unrecognized and maligned, in Dostoevsky's ability to enter into the minds of criminals, in R. D. Laing's sympathetic sense of what it means to be schizophrenic, and in the careful and penetrating reports of the Poor Law Commissioners in nineteenth-century England. Civility is manifest in Abraham Lincoln's awareness that his enemies in the South were human beings like the people of the North, fallible but in most cases doing what they thought was right. Such attentiveness expresses a concern for all human experience, an unwillingness that anything should remain unheard and unknown. Alexander Solzhenitsyn expresses the faith of civility when he says that "mankind's sole salvation lies in everyone making everything his business."[6]

The reflections contained in Chapter VII have prepared us for going further than this: communication is not confined to the living; comprehensive communality means being related, as far as possible, with all generations, with all of history.

Now, however, we can understand the idea more fully than we could at first. We can see historical communality as a personal stance—as the posture of a single human being contending against alienation, responding to the irresistible and uncontrollable tide of world events. Also, we can see historical communality as a basis both for detachment and for action. As for detachment, one who is linked even in tenuous ways with past and future ages, conscious even dimly of the vast temporal extent of the humanity in which he participates, is less dependent than he might otherwise be on his own society and his own time. In action, on the other hand, he is less at the mercy of historical conditions than would otherwise be the case; in a stance of historical communality, he is engaged not only in the always hazardous venture of trying to influence history but also in the task of trying to understand it in the communal setting provided by attentiveness to the past and availability to the future.

Historical communality is not something apart from participation in one's own polity and nation, however; it is rather the form that such

6. Quoted by Anthony Lewis, *New York Times*, January 6, 1973.

participation must take in order to have its proper value. The reflections on patriotism in Chapter VI were concerned with this idea. Historical communality becomes concrete through loyalty—perhaps paradoxical in quality, hence rebellious in expression—to a particular society.

As historical autonomy expresses a recognition that a desired historical change properly begins within one's own being, so comprehensive communality comes from a realization that a will to actual, outward community properly arises only from personal communality. The political idea of universal community is approached, not by trying through violence to transform the world, but by way of one's own resolute attentiveness.

It must be carefully noted, however, that being attentive is very different from being observant. Attentiveness is intersubjective and consequently looks for something more than explanation. Observation, like action, objectifies, and it comes to rest in explanation. The difference is illustrated in Marxism. There is little doubt that Marxist methodology helps to explain social and political behavior; it may be that no other theory has been so successful in this respect. But the very successes of Marxism have contributed to its overall failure: that it has not, as Marx intended, guided mankind into community. It is not just that the successes of Marxism have encouraged its followers to scorn all other theories, although that has happened and is part of the problem. These successes have encouraged Marxists to reject serious, inquiring discourse with non-Marxists. Many of Marx's followers have felt themselves able to explain completely why some people disagree with them and thus have felt no obligation to put themselves in the place of such people or to look seriously for truth in what they say. In this way Marxism has been destructive of communication and community. This has happened, I believe, because it has cultivated a purely observant and explanatory relationship among human beings and thus has undermined attentiveness.

The earlier discussions of recognition can throw some light on attentiveness. No recognition is implied in observing others, and no recognition is implied by even the fullest and most accurate explanation. Recognition means acknowledgment of something that is personal and thus invisible to a detached observer and theoretically inexplicable. Recognition can be expressed only in attentiveness.

Beyond attentiveness, however, comprehensive communality requires something else equally difficult, and that is availability, or a readiness to respond. I speak of availability, of a state of readiness, rather than of responding itself, because opportunities for responding are meager. Only a few of the most prominent political and cultural leaders can speak to great numbers of people; many have little opportunity to speak seriously to anyone. All that can be asked of most of us is that we be available to our "neighbor"—to the one whom we happen to encounter in a situation with communal possibilities.

At first it may seem that communality is the opposite of autonomy, and that the two cannot be combined. On reflection, however, it becomes clear that autonomy is possible only by virtue of a supreme relationship—one that renders every lesser relationship conditional. Universal communality can serve as that supreme relationship. Conversely, it becomes clear that universal communality entails autonomy. Comprehensive attentiveness and availability preclude total absorption in any particular relationship. In this way they dissolve the absolutist claims of ideologies and groups.

Therefore, it is not surprising that the ideal of an autonomy that is at the same time perfect communality is ancient and enduring. Examples are not only Plato's "Inner City," but also the Stoic "Cosmopolis," Augustine's "City of God," and Kant's "Kingdom of Ends." All are versions of the notion that to be perfectly at one with others is to be wholly independent, and that even in solitude a person may dwell within an ideal commonwealth.

At least one actual life evinces this solitary communality, that of Socrates. Socrates was cognizant of the fatal results for himself that his conversations, exposing the ignorance of Athenian leaders, might have, but he carried them on until he was silenced by the executioner. Not even the threat of death induced him to limit his autonomy; yet that autonomy was nothing but a defiant communality.

The third element in civility is at once in conflict with and an inescapable manifestation of communality.

3. EXEMPLARY ACTION. The problem presented by the ideal of civility is to find a way of acting that expresses man's communal nature and at the same time gives significance to what is done by a single individual—by one whose influence on the course of history must be as

insignificant as that of a drop of rainwater on a river. The answer, I suggest, is that one should act for all, in the sense of doing that which all, or all within a certain category, ought to do. Solidarity and independence, in this way, are affirmed simultaneously.

Exemplary action might take a variety of forms. It might be conceived of as action that all should emulate, such as refusing to obey an unjust law; it might in its nature be confined to a few and carried out in secret, as would be the case, for example, with an attempt to sabotage an industry contributing to a genocidal war. What makes an action exemplary is that it is conceived from the standpoint not just of probable consequences but of whether, immediately or eventually, it can suitably be commended to public attention. An exemplary action is fitted to serve as a statement of principle.

Exemplary action embodies the standards both of autonomy and of communality. It embodies the standard of autonomy in two ways. It can be undertaken on the initiative of a single individual and is not contingent on the cooperation of others. Further, although calling for a realistic calculation of consequences, it frees the agent from the incubus that weighs always on an individual in his political life: that what he does can have only a negligible effect on the world and history. Whatever the consequences, exemplary action in itself is an affirmation of solidarity and is that far saved from futility.

Exemplary action embodies the standard of communality because it is expressive. It is action as a form of address. This is true even if the agent is the only one attentive to the act, indeed even if the act must by its nature be done in secret. The agent in this case acts in the public realm of his own inner city.

The whole concept of civility can now be summarily restated. Civility means living according to the demands of the humanity that one recognizes in others and finds in one's own identity; it means doing this through historical autonomy, all-inclusive communality, and exemplary action. There is an old concept, discussed earlier in these reflections, that connotes much of what we are here concerned with. That is the concept of tolerance. To be tolerant is to be in some measure communal (not merely indifferent, as was brought out in Chapter V), for the other person is granted freedom to speak honestly and be heard. It is also to be autonomous, because granting freedom to ideologies and groups to which one is opposed presupposes a loosening of one's own ideological and group commitments.

The development of tolerance in the seventeenth and eighteenth centuries was a historical achievement not only because it ended the slaughter of the religious wars but also because it opened up the possibility of civil life. The religious dogmatism and uniformity of the Middle Ages and Reformation made civility impossible. It was not religious faith as such that did this but the identification of faith with acceptance of a single doctrine and a single set of institutions. But the civility implicit in tolerance was far from wholly realized. After the beginning of the industrial revolution, the bourgeoisie proved to be highly uncivil; and the revolt against bourgeois incivility, led by Marx, gave rise to new dogmas. Also, with the waning of religious faith leading into the spiritual vacuum of the twentieth century, tolerance has tended to fade into apathy. In any case, the establishment of tolerance was more than an enhancement of the basic decencies of life. It made accessible modes of relatedness, and thus of being human, that had been largely closed off since the end of antiquity.

While civility is a relationship, it is also a way of being oneself. It might be characterized as self-transcendence. Recent thinkers have argued that a person establishes his identity through his actions and that sentiments unexpressed in action, far from constituting the real self, are actually of no significance. This argument is valuable as a counterweight to the easy and sentimental notion that a person cannot be known as he really is through the many unworthy acts he has committed, but only through the beautiful feelings that are unexpressed in his observable life. It seems to me, nevertheless, that it is as arbitrary wholly to identify a person with his acts as it is wholly to identify him with the inner regrets and hopes in which those acts are transcended. The concept of civility, calling on us to act in a self-critical and tentative fashion, sanctions the idea that selfhood lies both in that which is transcended and in that which transcends.

This is an issue in which a good deal is at stake. The principle that selfhood is determined wholly by action has destructive consequences. Having made a decision, one would have to act, so to speak, with eyes closed; doubt and reconsideration would be impossible, and repentance would be impossible. There could be no communication, for communication cannot be fully serious without deliberately risking the established self. Tolerance would be barred since it depends on acknowledging that one's own acts and beliefs may legitimately be called into question. Much that we value depends on self-transcendence.

The philosophical basis of this paradoxical concept of personal identity is the philosophical basis of civility itself—the twofold nature of man. A human being is both a product of history and a source of history; in relation to others he is a means and is also an end in himself. Hence to live as a human being and with human beings is continually to be entangled in contradictions. Civility is an effort not to escape from such contradictions, but to accept them and to turn them into sources of vital tension.

Civility is in many ways a departure from contemporary attitudes and ideas. For example, it means eschewing "engagement," or at least the kind of unconditional commitments that have been glorified in recent years. If every commitment is to some finite and imperfect historical entity, then it is surely appropriate that political choices be tentative and regretful. In some circumstances, of course, an irreversible and unreserved commitment may be inescapable. Have we not tended, however, to make this kind of commitment the norm and thus dangerously to sentimentalize the conditions of political life? The idea of cutting free from doubt and being totally committed has a powerful appeal. But this appeal may derive from our craving for a status beyond the imperfections around us and the perfectly appropriate hesitations within us.

Civility entails an ideological detachment that intellectuals are apt to disapprove of and even find incomprehensible. Thus, to be civil is to be respectful of tradition and inclined to acquiesce in the demands of authority (since civilization depends on tradition and authority), yet not to be a conservative. To be civil is to realize that it is in the nature of society to dehumanize its members, and that society needs to be opposed and probably occasionally to be forcibly reorganized, yet not to be a radical. To be civil is to prize liberty, yet, assuming that liberalism is another ideology alongside conservatism and radicalism, not to be a liberal.

The idea of civility also breaks with contemporary thought with respect to personal happiness. It is often held, even by thinkers of the stature of Hannah Arendt, that conscientious citizenship is a way to happiness.[7] The standard of civility, however, prescribes a taxing and uncomfortable posture, a posture befitting man but unlikely to produce anything as relatively simple and superficial as happiness. Thus civility entails responsibility of a kind that cannot be laid to rest with a few sweeping decisions but that involves one in recurrent crises of reconsideration. Civility spells alienation; this is implicit in the refusal of identification with any group or program of action. Civility is inseparable from insecurity, since it requires one to do without either theoretical assurance or unequivocal social and political identity. Finally, civility carries with it a sense of powerlessness, because the average individual can have only a negligible influence on the course of history, and to feel powerless is to feel superfluous—not just in general but precisely in one's civility; it would not matter to the world if one ceased being civil.

This is a long way from the "public happiness" that Hannah Arendt finds in the public realm. I do not mean to say that there is no happiness at all in civility, much less that there is no satisfaction of any kind. However, in the age of Hitler and Stalin, of the Hiroshima bombing and the war in Vietnam, to delineate prospects of public happiness through political action is to indulge in fantasies.

It may be seen that civility, however, is too near the opposite pole from most of our fantasies—that it expresses an extreme historical pessimism. This impression might call forth several objections that deserve to be considered and answered.

Civility and Hope

It can be argued, either on humanistic or on religious grounds, that despair is wrong even where it is not demonstrably in error. It is destructive, tending in itself to produce the results anticipated. Hope, then, might be regarded as an obligation—an obligation insufficiently recognized in the concept of civility.

It is true that the concept of civility is formed by the disappointments and disasters of our history. It tells us that history is not within the scope of our knowledge or command. But it does not call on us to

7. See, for example, Hannah Arendt, *On Revolution* (New York: The Viking Press, 1963), where the concept of public happiness is discussed.

become doctrinaire pessimists. That would be to change the content of our error without giving it up. To hold that history *must* be disastrous and that overall progress *cannot* occur evinces pride—not the exuberant pride often associated with the doctrine of progress but the despairing pride of using cynicism as a shield against disappointment. Civility requires historical openness, and that is different from relying on history to be either benign or malignant.

This is to speak of theoretical presuppositions. As for actual results, civility might paradoxically turn out to be more beneficial than revolutionary determination. Radicals are morally outraged by anyone who is not resolved to uproot all of the evil in human society. They should remember, however, that those men in our time who have dedicated themselves to the total eradication of evil have not merely failed; they have, in many cases, themselves become major sources of evil. Revolutionary determination has not so far proven to be historically beneficial.

The concept of civility sanctions hesitation and regret, and this offers another possible object of criticism. It may seem that civility is contrary to the decisiveness that is often needed in affairs of state. It appears, for example, that indecision, resulting in numerous halfway measures, contributed to the tragic American involvement in Vietnam.[8] One might ask whether civility does not have an inherent tendency to produce such results.

What civility calls for, however, is not drift but self-transcendence. That these are not the same and do not necessarily go together is shown by the example of Lincoln. There is no question of Lincoln's capacity for facing issues and making difficult decisions. Had the nation been permitted to drift in 1861, it would have broken apart. Yet Lincoln was also able to look at himself from a distance. His civility is manifest in his persistent sense that not only his opponents, but he, too, was under the judgment of God.

Perhaps the most disturbing characteristic of civility, however, is that it implies a certain resignation to injustice—not merely for oneself, which might seem morally admissible, but for others. Thus a comfortably situated professor, practicing civility, may come to terms with the prospect that most human beings, for generations or even always, will

8. For evidence of this, see David Halberstam, *The Best and the Brightest* (New York: Random House, 1972).

live in physical squalor. It might be charged, accordingly, that civility is little more than a euphemism for complacency.

A suspicion of this sort cannot be dismissed. It pertains, however, not to civility alone but to every moral posture. No doubt civility may be used as a mask for complacency, perhaps deceiving even the one using it; but the determination to uproot injustice may be a mask for self-righteousness and resentment. As Reinhold Niebuhr pointed out, radicals are often naïvely unaware of the moral ambiguities in their own behavior, even though, aided by Marxist insights, they are often highly sensitive to such ambiguities in the behavior of others. This naïve self-assurance has, of course, not been a mere peccadillo. It has given rise to despotism and bloodshed, and it has done this to such a degree that it might be reasonably argued that radicals have done less to diminish injustice in the world than have those whose opposition to injustice has been tempered by a measure of historical resignation.

Still, leaving hidden motives aside, is it not right to oppose injustice? It cannot be denied that it is and that radicalism realizes a formal and sometimes heroic rectitude. The respect owed to this rectitude is suggested by its presence not only in Marx and other modern radicals, but also in the prophets of the Old Testament. They too were outraged by injustice and by acquiescence in injustice. How, then, can such acquiescence in any form or degree be defended as civil?

As moral will, it cannot. As an assessment of historical prospects, however, it may simply be an acknowledgment of reality. One may be deeply and rightly incensed by prevailing injustices; it is simply false, nevertheless, to forecast their imminent end. We have no grounds for doing so, and anyone who urges us to bolster our determination by cultivating the faith that what *should* certainly *will* come to pass offers dubious advice. It is dubious not only in its carelessness of the truth, but pragmatically as well; as many of our hardest experiences show, confidence in the future is not necessarily benign.

The truth is simply that what we are morally bound to will and what we can reasonably expect are not always the same. Radicals and conservatives typically join in finding this contradiction insupportable, with the former adjusting expectations to will and the latter will to expectations. If the idea of civility is valid, however, then the contradiction between morality and history is one source of the tensions inherent in realizing one's historicity. Clearly it is not easy to will one thing and to anticipate something else. Kant's moral writings, however, have familiarized us with such a position and seem to show that it is not psychologically impossible. At bottom, to say that will and expectation must be incongruous is only to point to the necessity for self-transcendence.

One way in which Americans might reflect on the historical implications of activist self-confidence, in comparison with civility, is by considering what has happened to them in Vietnam. That experience may plausibly be interpreted as a tragedy of incivility. If American involvement in Vietnam had a primary spiritual source, this seems to have been the assurance that history was under American control. This assurance was apparently associated with a multifaceted pride: nationalistic pride, in which it was taken for granted that America, with its restless genius and its unparalleled power, could not possibly be thwarted by a tiny peasant people in Asia; intellectual pride, evident in the confidence that "sheer intelligence and rationality could answer and solve anything";[9] pride of youth, present in a young president with many young advisers; and pride of experience and class, present in leaders of the foreign policy establishment who were serenely sure that they could wisely direct America's course in world affairs. It is noteworthy that this spirit of historical dominion had ideological manifestations, above all anticommunism and the doctrine of containment.

It goes without saying that historical events are complex and that the mood I am characterizing was not the exclusive source of American actions in Vietnam. But it is unlikely that we would ever have become so resolutely committed to a cause bearing so slightly on our national interests had it not been for an extraordinary confidence in our powers of action. One observer of the period during which this commitment was being forged remarks that a "remarkable hubris permeated this entire time."[10]

Civility does not mean giving up all hope; it only means refusing to rely on man and his command of events. But it is where assurance of

9. *Ibid.*, 44.
10. *Ibid.*, 123.

historical command is at its height that there is most to fear. In a more civil world there would be—and there would be justification for—modest hope.

Regardless of its implications for history, however, one may feel that civility is too difficult and grim for the individual. It is widely assumed today that life should be agreeable and that anyone who does not find it so must be guilty of mismanagement, a victim of some unique misfortune, or else psychologically unsettled. As I have pointed out, the standard of civility does not wholly accord with this outlook. It prescribes trying responsibilities and leads to alienation. One cannot resolve to be civil and still remain free to live just as he likes. One cannot expect civility to open the way into that uncomplicated and satisfied state of mind that is usually called "happiness."

Nevertheless, civility is perhaps not so difficult, or at least not so exceptional, as one might suppose. Do not many ordinary people look skeptically on ideologies and on the promises of leaders, view the future with misgivings, and still try to keep in touch with affairs, to consider sympathetically the problems of other people, and to meet their political responsibilities? So far as they do, they achieve something like civility. It is rather intellectuals, perhaps, who involve themselves in more dramatic commitments, or at least feel that they should. Intellectuals are perhaps more troubled than others by the intellectually humbling notion that no existing, or even possible, ideology is altogether true; engaged in the enterprise of noetic mastery, they may be particularly inclined to assume the possibility of practical mastery; and once they lose confidence in the future they may be more likely than those who are less thoughtful to draw the seemingly logical, although erroneous, conclusion that one may as well abandon all political responsibility. This should not be taken to mean that civility is no more than common sense, but only that its paradoxes, although particularly disturbing to those habituated to thought and logic, do not seem to place intolerable demands on human balance.

Moreover, what is difficult and grim in civility is not gratuitous. It is the burden of sharing existence with billions of beings who are infinitely mysterious, who are sometimes kindly and sometimes cruel, each of whom has a claim to be treated as an end and not merely as a means. There is no way in which that situation can be made easy and pleasant.

Civility was defined above in terms of tolerance, and it is noteworthy that the word *tolerance* derives from Latin words meaning *to lift up*, or *to bear*. This suggests that civility is the stance in which one consciously bears, in the sense both of enduring and of supporting, the existence of multitudes of unpredictable and troublesome fellow humans.

In pursuance of this line of thought, it may be suggested that the modern emphasis on historical results is an effort to escape from beneath this burden of plurality. A great deal has been done to meet the threats of nature through intelligent mastery. It is not surprising that men should strive in the same way to meet the threats arising from one another. But as soon as the idea is stated, we see its mortal error: to seek intelligent mastery of human beings is to treat them as means and to preclude community. The standard of civility calls on us to maintain the integrity of our communal nature even in the face of the communal disasters of our time.

It should also be said, however, that civility is not all grimness. The proposition that civility cannot be expected to produce happiness does not imply that it must result simply in unhappiness. Civility is an effort to take part in history while avoiding political idolatry, to achieve a universal relatedness that is uncorrupted either by absolutism in theory or fanaticism in action. It means trying to participate in the affairs of the whole human race without either killing in order to redeem the earth from all evil or pretending that established society, with all of its subtle and habitual as well as glaring injustices, is a community. Is it not possible that in thus acknowledging at once the calamitous imperfection of everything historical and the immeasurable dignity of the human— in taking a position befitting at once the historical and the moral dimensions of our existence—something may be found that is better than happiness?